# SIP *by* SIP

# SIP *by* SIP

*An Insider's Guide to Learning*
*All About Wine*

# Michael Bonadies

Doubleday

*New York London Toronto Sydney Auckland*

*Dedicated to*
*Nick ('88), Joe ('90), and Tony ('95)*
*My Favorite Vintages*

PUBLISHED BY DOUBLEDAY
a division of Bantam Doubleday Dell Publishing Group, Inc.
1540 Broadway, New York, New York 10036

DOUBLEDAY and the portrayal of an anchor with a dolphin are trademarks of Doubleday, a division of Bantam Doubleday Dell Publishing Group, Inc.

Some of the material in this book has appeared previously in *Wine & Spirits* magazine.

BOOK DESIGN BY RENATO STANISIC

Library of Congress Cataloging-in-Publication Data
Bonadies, Michael.
    Sip by sip: an insider's guide to learning all about wine / Michael Bonadies.—1st ed.
      p.     cm.
    Includes index.
    1. Wine and wine making.  I. Title.
  TP548.B69    1998
  641.2′2—dc21
                                    98-16924
                                    CIP

# Acknowledgments

I could not have written this book without the help, inspiration, and encouragement of countless people. I want to thank everyone who has shared their knowledge with me: the many authors and writers whose books and articles on wine first fed my thirst for learning; the winemakers—Jim Clendenen, Rob Davis, Burt Williams, and Craig Williams—who have over the years patiently answered my questions; and my colleagues—David Gordon, Daniel Johnnes, Tim Kopec, and Larry Stone—who have always been generous in sharing their wealth of wine knowledge and expertise with me.

I want to thank everyone who has inspired me to write this book: the thousands and thousands of wonderful customers who patronize the Myriad restaurants and whose interest in wine was a key catalyst in writing this book; my family and friends, who are always full of questions about wine; and all of the Myriad Restaurant Group servers—in particular, David DeBacco, Adrienne Elder, and Jennifer Ely—who each played important roles in the creation of this book.

I would be terribly remiss if I didn't thank everyone who has ever shared a bottle of wine with me, especially Joe Phelps, who has always encouraged and supported me and who, in response to my persistent badgering as to how he learned all about wine, replied with a wry smile, "Sip by sip."

This book could not have been written without the help and encouragement of my partners Drew Nieporent and Martin Shapiro; fellow wine lovers Jean Arnold, Josh Green,

Bob Lescher, Tom Shelton, Diane and Levon Soorikian, and Carlo Russo; and especially my terrific and very patient editors at Doubleday, Judy Kern and Bob Daniels.

Finally, I want to thank the most important people in my life, my family: my grandparents, Florence and Rocco Bonadies and Greba and Fred Graper, who taught me the love of food and a good story; my parents, Kathleen and Daniel Bonadies, whose faith in my abilities has never wavered; my three sons, Nick, Joe, and Tony, whose incredible energy, curiosity, and love fuel my dreams; and most important, my beautiful wife, Anne, who inspires me, who makes it possible for me to write, and who has taught me the true meaning of being a writer, father, and husband. Thank you.

# Contents

# Introduction

Early in my restaurant wine career, I asked Joe Phelps, owner and founder of his own Napa Valley winery, how he came to know and enjoy wine. Raised on the saints and their piercing revelations, I desperately sought confirmation that I was choosing the right vocation.

There I was, my friends all making *real* money from real jobs on Wall Street, in law, in advertising, and in publishing. I was torn by doubt, my faith wavering. Wine was *too* much fun. It gave pleasure. It was something my Midwestern, Protestant, teetotaling grandmother positively disapproved of. I waited anxiously as Joe sat across the table sipping his wine. Finally, with a wry smile, he replied, "Sip by sip."

While not exactly a Zen riddle, his answer clearly lacked the dramatic clarity I sought. Sipping my wine, staring blankly at the menu, I consoled myself with how wonderful the wine tasted and tried to remember what my LSAT scores had been. Was it too late for a real job?

Years later, as I sit here writing this book, I realize Joe was right. There was no shortcut. No utter certainty. Just lots of fun as I tasted my way, sip by sip, to the most fulfilling vocation I could have chosen.

Wine is fun—fun to drink, fun to learn about, and fun to share. It tastes good too. But since most of us in this country haven't grown up with wine, we must overcome the twin obstacles of fear and humiliation before wine really becomes fun. *How to Banish Fear (And Make Wine Fun)* could just as easily have been the title of this book. I remember the terrorizing fear of being confronted with a winelist the size of a phone directory and a smirking sommelier who knew I could barely pronounce Chardonnay, and of being cornered in a wineshop by a salesman who gleefully pointed out my ignorance of malolactic fermentation while cheerfully humiliating me into spending $25 for a bottle when my budget was $4.95. And let's not forget the know-it-all brother-in-law who, rather than encourage my new interest in wine, looked down his nose at every bottle I so proudly brought over for dinner. Sound familiar? Novice, intermediate, or expert—it has happened to us all.

The key to banishing any and all fear of wine is to develop your own taste and then build confidence in that taste. The goal of this book is to help you become more confident and knowledgeable about what you like and enjoy about wine. There are no shortcuts, no magic bullets, no high-tech marvels when it comes to wine. Only the old-fashioned method of sitting down with a bottle and a glass and learning, one sip at a time. It is hard work, but then again you could be studying organic chemistry.

The focus of this book, without apology, is on California. There are ten reasons for this:

1. I am an unabashed California wine chauvinist. Proudly so. Some of the world's greatest wine is being made in California right now.
2. The French make great wine, no doubt. But Californians are a hell of a lot more fun. Ever try to surf in France?
3. A translator isn't usually required to converse with a Californian, although being able to discuss your previous lives can help.
4. California wines probably represent the single biggest selection in your local wineshop and on the winelist of your favorite restaurant.
5. The weather is better in California.
6. Anything and everything grows in California. Which means just about every single important variety of grape in the world grows and is vinified in California today, and is thus available for discussion in this book.
7. I would never finish writing this book otherwise.
8. The most exciting, adventurous strides in viticulture and winemaking are taking place in California.
9. I was born in California but grew up in Connecticut and have never forgiven my parents for moving.
10. The sequel: "Sip by Sip Goes to France."

I have learned (and forgotten) a lot about wine during my years in the restaurant business. Probably the most important thing I learned was the danger of becoming an expert.

Once upon a time, on the verge of becoming a wine expert, I suddenly discovered that wine was no longer fun. I had become too critical. I was tasting every wine looking for faults rather than pleasure. Even my kids were swirling their milk and discussing its bouquet. Luckily, I was able to regain my amateur status. So I write this book not as a wine expert but as a winelover, hoping to share my passion for wine in an attempt to tempt, cajole, lure, and urge you into a grand adventure.

Wine is still fun for me. After years of sipping, I am still learning. Now I hope to share with you some of what I have learned. Good luck and happy sipping.

—MICHAEL BONADIES

# First Sips and Other Tall Tales

Do you remember your very first sip, that first gag-me/ethereal/boring/tentative/grin-and-bear-it/euphoric/religious/stolen/underage (circle one or more) sip? I remember my first sip. It was a stolen gulp of Uncle John's homemade red. The inky, viscous stuff—a close first cousin to antifreeze—went no farther than my tongue. My eight-year-old palate, finely honed on gallons of Mountain Dew, rebelled. I expelled the pride and joy of my great-uncle's basement all over my new Sunday shoes.

My first bona fide swallow of wine—now that was a different matter altogether. It involved a black '69 GTO with a jacked-up rear end and mag wheels, Santana blaring on the radio, and a paper-bagged bottle of Boone's Farm Apple Wine. Oh, and a carload of sixteen-year-old boys. Cliché—yes. Dangerous—absolutely. But it was fun.

1. What was your first sip of wine? _____
2. Was it _____
   a) white?
   b) pink?
   c) red?
   d) Day-Glo?
3. Was it: _____
   a) sweet?
   b) bitter?
   c) fizzy?
4. Did you pronounce it correctly? _____
5. Did it have a screw top? _____

6. Was it part of a religious ceremony? _____

7. Or did you succumb to peer pressure? _____

8. Did you swallow? _____

9. Did it lead to: _____

    a) wild sex?

    b) semi-wild sex?

    c) fantasies of any kind of sex?

10. Did the earth move (or just spin)? _____

11. Did you respect yourself in the morning? _____

12. Were you of legal drinking age? _____

13. Were you fraught with performance anxiety about: _____

    a) how far to tip the chalice?

    b) how to describe its aromas and flavors?

    c) what to do as the brown paper bag began to disintegrate from the condensation?

    d) where to spit it out?

14. Was your first food-and-wine pairing with a controlled substance in the hemp family? _____

15. Have you at this time or at any other lied about your first sip? _____

Whether your first sip was Boone's Farm, White Zinfandel, Ripple, Bartles & Jaymes, Manischewitz, Mad Dog 20-20, or even Dom Pérignon, it was merely the start of what can be a lifelong exploration filled with fun and adventure, pleasure and surprise. The key word here is "fun." If you're not having as much fun with wine as you should, it is probably because of wine snobs (aka wine geeks, cork dorks, and brothers-in-law) and wine myths. Wine snobs will be dealt with over the course of this book as your knowledge and confidence grow, but wine myths need to be tackled immediately.

# WINE MYTHS

The myths of Zeus, Thor, Oedipus, King Arthur, and Pecos Bill arose out of a society's need to explain its world or a specific phenomenon of its world. These same myths, in some cases after thousands of years, continue to offer insight as well as to entertain. So why do myths exist about wine?

There are three reasons why wine myths have currency in the United States:

1. Wine remains a "foreign" beverage, not part of our American upbringing or culture. And as such, it remains mysterious and a subject of myth.
2. Wine myths foster the elitism and sense of secret knowledge that wine snobs thrive on.
3. Wine myths enable everyone in the business of selling wine to charge more for their product.

So if there are kernels of truth in the ancient myths that keep us trying to decipher them, what about wine myths? Are there any self-evident truths lurking in these tales? Let's see.

## Myth #1: Expensive Is Better/Cheaper Is Better

There are two dramatically opposed and fervently believed myths on price: 1) expensive is better (pure snobbery), and 2) cheaper is better (reverse snobbery). Slavish adherence to either myth limits your options and fun. The big-bucks school confines you to the big names and might blind you to discovering a great $9 bottle of Zinfandel or Merlot or Sauvignon Blanc. Subscribe solely to the bargain-basement school and you'll never know the thrill of splurging for a great bottle.

Price, high or low, is an accurate indicator neither of quality nor of value. A high price can be an indicator of hype, limited availability, speculation, or greed. But a low price doesn't guarantee value either. The measure of value is the sensual pleasure that a wine is able to deliver. If a $9 bottle delivers at least nine bucks of pleasure, you're way ahead of the game. If a $900 bottle delivers at least nine hundred bucks of pleasure and enjoyment, you've gotten your money's worth. But a word of caution: Beware of the rising expectations that can be created by a price tag. Throw your monthly budget out the window, splurge for that $900 bottle, and you may find yourself wanting it be so wonderful that it has no chance in hell of living up to your expectations.

***Bottom Line:*** Don't be afraid to splurge, and don't be shy about bargain hunting. Just remember that price, like taste, is entirely relative. What is expensive today might be cheap next week after you win $10 million in the lottery. At $9 or $900, it still gets flushed down the toilet the next morning.

# You Talking to Me?

*Atmospheresabboccatoacetalhehydeanthocyansautovinificationbentonitebacksbeutel-brettanomycesbrix—you talking to me? Fuggedabowdit. There's no need to understand or use jargon to enjoy wine. Don't let a bunch of gibberish intimidate you for a second.*

### Myth #2: French Is Better

Yeah, right.

**Bottom Line:** Don't limit yourself to only one country or region. Explore the entire world of wine and all the fun and pleasure it has to offer.

### Myth #3: Pronunciation Matters

Does a wine taste any better if you pronounce it correctly? I am phonetically challenged. My French is terrible. My Italian, German, and Spanish are even worse. Do I care? No.

**Bottom Line:** Never hesitate to order a bottle of wine because of a lack of language fluency or fear of pronunciation. Do what I do: Point or use the bin number, gleefully butcher the pronunciation, and get the wine you want.

### Myth #4: Cellar Size Matters

Is bigger better? Is this a question anyone (except for those with a big cellar) ever answers truthfully? Let's be honest. Bigger is better. It is fun to collect and build a cellar. But it is critical to have a collecting strategy tailored to your taste, lifestyle, and wallet. The last thing you want is to end up with a cellar full of wine that you don't like, that you can never find the right occasion to drink, or that pushes your credit cards past their limit.

**Bottom Line:** Whether you have a single-case cellar in a closet or a 10-case cellar in the basement or a 1,000-case high-tech marvel of a cellar, what matters most is that you drink, share, and enjoy the wine you purchase. And remember a motto to live by: "He who dies with the most wine loses."

### Myth #5: Technique Is More Important Than Size

Only for those with small cellars. But let's take a look at technique anyway.

***Serving Temperature:*** The serving temperature is important because it affects the wine's taste. The problem in this country is that, on the whole, white wine is served too cold and red wine too warm. A frigid white loses its complexity of aroma and flavor. A warm red smells and tastes too much of alcohol, and its charm and pleasure are obscured. If you don't believe me, try the following experiment: Chill a bottle of white wine in an ice bucket or freezer until it is frigid to the touch. Open it and try a taste. Leave the bottle out on the counter and then every ten minutes pour a fresh taste. As the wine "warms," it will begin to develop greater complexity of aroma and flavor and, in short, taste better. (Don't try heating up a red, because you could easily ruin the wine.)

So what's the ideal serving temperature for red wine: Cellar temperature? Room temperature? Fifty-five to 65 degrees? Let's be realistic here. Unless you're lucky, or have spent some bucks, the "cellar" that stores your red wine is probably a little too warm (touch the bottle and see). This can be easily "fixed" by placing the bottle in the fridge for fifteen minutes, or until it is slightly cool to the touch before serving.

White wine should be served cold, but not Arctic-blast cold. If your refrigerator is perfect for beer, it is probably a little too cold for white wine. If the bottle is ice-cold, allow it to stand ten to fifteen minutes outside the refrigerator before serving. You'll learn to use your own sense of touch to discover the temperatures you find most enjoyable for whites and reds. With practice, you'll soon be able to touch a bottle of wine and know if the temperature is just right for your taste. So don't worry about the articles and books that list ideal temperatures for each and every kind of wine. Life's way too short to worry over every bottle's temperature, and there's too much good wine to drink.

***Opening the Bottle:*** Now that you've got the touchy-feely part down pat, your challenge is to liberate the wine. In a world of consumer-friendly packaging—flip tops, screw tops, pop tops, and zip locks—most wines require what looks like a medieval instrument of torture guaranteed to extract confessions from heretics.

Unfortunately, the success rates for corkscrews, even in the most practiced hands, is far from perfect. Corks are not a zero-defect product. They have a tendency to break, crumble, split, and slip back into the bottle. It's enough to make you reach for a beer. See page 184 for recommendations on corkscrews and how to use them, and pages 185–86 for what to do if the cork fails to cooperate.

***Heavy Breathing:*** What was your wine doing that it needs to breathe? Fifty push-ups? If air were a magic elixir for wine, there wouldn't be a cork stuck tight in the neck of the bottle, working full-time to keep it out. Open the bottle and pour. Over the course of drinking the bottle, you will notice that the wine evolves in the glass.

***Decanting:*** You'll need a decanter when you are drinking an older red wine or an unfined and unfiltered wine that has thrown sediment. How do you know if the bottle contains sediment? Pick the bottle up and hold it in front of a strong light. If the bottle has been standing up, you will see a dark ring of sediment at the bottom. If it has been lying on its side, you will see a swirling cloud of sediment when you lift it upright. In the second instance, stand the bottle upright, allowing the sediment to settle to the bottom before decanting. See pages 188–89 for instructions on how to properly decant.

***Glassware:*** Glassware definitely counts. Wine does taste better in relatively large hand-blown glasses.

***To Swirl or Not to Swirl:*** Swirling the wine helps release its aromas and is perfectly correct, as long as you don't swirl too vigorously and stain the tablecloth.

Q: When do you know that you've become a wine fanatic?

A: When your kids start swirling their milk.

***Bottom Line:*** Don't get hung up on technique. As long as you can get the wine out of the bottle and into the glass, you're ahead of the game.

## Myth #6: Old Wines Do It Better

Says who? The British. Our obsession with the mysterious wonders of old wines is due mainly to the influence British wine writers have had on wine experts in this country. The British prefer their wines old, if not dead and buried. This unseemly bent toward necrophilia certainly leaves an unpleasant taste, as many old wines disappoint. Why?

1. Ninety-five percent of the wine produced every year is meant for immediate consumption—bottoms up and down the hatch within a year of its release to the marketplace.

2. The remaining 5% is considered age-worthy because of track record, grape variety, style, or the vintner's ego.

3. When you read of incredibly wonderful bottles of old wine, and they do exist, what you do not read is that many exactly similar bottles have become tired, faded, and undrinkable.

4. Price, rarity, and age affect our perception, whether we are novice or expert. If a bottle is worth $1,000 or is incredibly rare (most old wines are both

expensive and rare), you are going to give it the benefit of the doubt. You want it to taste good—and if not actually good, at least interesting. And that is exactly what most old wines deliver: interest, not pleasure and joy.

5. Market forces help to support the myth that old wines do it better. Too many people have money invested in old wines, or young wines that will be worth a lot of money when they get old, for them to ever let go of this myth.

6. The biggest problem with old wines is storage. Where have they been during their long lives, and how have they been stored? If stored properly, they have a chance to be drinkable, if not very good; if stored improperly, they're probably vinegar or have faded.

So, what's old? If you want to be safe, any whites over five years old and reds over ten years old.

**Bottom Line:** Most wines are ready to drink on release, with younger wines tending to offer more obvious and immediate drinking pleasure. However, if you do become interested in collecting and drinking age-worthy reds, your best bet is to buy by the case soon after their release. Drink the wine over the next ten to fifteen years and keep notes on how it ages and evolves from your first bottle until your last. Following their release, drink age-worthy whites over the next five to eight years. And remember when buying wines that already have some age: their window of drinkability is going to be shorter.

## Myth #7: Vintage Counts

Hope springs eternal every spring in the hearts of California vintners. Starting with bud break in the vineyards, vintners fantasize about perfect weather, a flawless harvest, and the vintage of the century. And since weather is the primary determinant of whether a specific vintage will be judged great, terrible, or so-so, California has an advantage when it comes to vintage. Because of its consistently good weather for grapes, there are relatively few bad vintages in California. As a result, vintage is often not a tremendously important topic of discussion when it comes to California wines. This is not to say that there are not certain vintages in California that are superior to others, but the odds are that whenever you purchase a bottle of California wine, the vintage on the label will be pretty good to excellent.

The same is not true for Bordeaux, California's main competitor when it comes to

# EXCEPTION TO THE RULE

*Madeira lives nearly forever. The fortified wine that takes its name from its island birthplace, Madeira was once the favored drink of George Washington, Thomas Jefferson, and Daniel Webster. Today, it is the longest-living wine. But that's because it undergoes a semipasteurization (it is literally "cooked" in heated lodges), which, together with the wine's amazing acidity, ensures long life. Madeiras from the 1800s are still delicious, as my tasting notes on the Bual Solera 1845, Cossart, Gordon, show: "Produced at the height of Madeira's popularity, this wine has survived Madeira's decline into near oblivion in the American market. One hundred and fifty-three years old, it possesses a youthful, dark amber color. While its earthy aromas of chocolate, citrus, and coffee intrigue, the first sip is not only a taste of history but a revelation. The subtle aromas have failed to prepare me for the power, intensity, and length this wine delivers with each taste. The caramel, spice, nut, and citrus flavors are not only fresh and youthful, but they seem to last forever on the finish."*

Cabernet Sauvignon– and Merlot–based wines. Bordeaux has lousy weather. The climate is far more marginal and fickle. The grapes struggle to ripen, and rain often strikes during harvest. Consequently, vintage is very important in the discussion or purchase of Bordeaux wines.

**Bottom Line:** Vintage counts if you are: 1) cellaring specific vintages because of your children's birth years, or 2) buying wine (particularly Bordeaux) for the purpose of financial investment. Otherwise, be careful—vintage is often used unscrupulously as a marketing tool.

## Myth #8: Scores Count Even More

Wine magazines keep score. And with the thousands of wines available on the marketplace in every category and at every price, point scores can be a helpful guide. But one note of caution. Most wine scores are arrived at by committee. Wines are judged at tastings held by panels who collectively score the wines. Having participated in a fair share of tasting panels, I must confess the following:

1. Halfway through thirty young Cabernets, all I could think of was a cold beer.
2. Some of the wines I loved everyone else hated.
3. Some of the wines I hated everyone else loved.
4. And some wines half of us loved, while the other half hated.
5. When you taste that many wines at one sitting, you end up tasting for faults and flaws rather than pleasure. The tendency is to favor power over elegance. And it is clear that your critical faculties are much sharper, and thus fairer, with the first few wines than with the last few.

**Bottom Line:** Your own sense of taste is not arrived at by committee. Consequently, in order to use scores as a more effective buying guide, it's best to find an individual wine critic to follow. Now you'll be dealing with one person's taste, not the averaged taste of a panel. Robert Parker, Jr., who publishes *The Wine Advocate,* immediately comes to mind. Buy several wines he scores highly and try them. Do you like the wines as much as he does? If not, try Steve Tanzer, who publishes the *International Wine Cellar.* And if that fails too, you just might by now have a pretty good idea of what you do like, as well as what you clearly don't.

### Myth #9: Food and Wine

Food and wine were made to go together. It's that simple. Why do people try to complicate matters by making such a fuss about pairing exactly the right wine with the right food.

# EL NIÑO

*It never rains in sunny California except when El Niño hits. El Niño, a global climatic effect caused by a large mass of unusually warm water in the Pacific Ocean, brings winter rains to the California wine country. The winter of 1997–98 saw El Niño slam California with heavy rains and flooding, which caused millions of dollars of damage. Fortunately, the grape vines were dormant during the winter and the rains had little negative effect. El Niño's adverse effect on a vineyard is very specific, and limited to erosion or flood damage caused when water-borne debris strikes individual vines. If anything, El Niño's rains are a positive, as they fill the reservoirs, recharge the soil's ability to retain water, and keep it cool, paving the way for a long growing season and a potentially excellent vintage.*

**Bottom Line:** Don't lose any sleep over pairing food and wine. Drink what you like, eat what you like, and concentrate on enjoying yourself. Life's too short to waste a single second agonizing over the perfect food-and-wine match. It doesn't exist. But most of the matches you make by drinking and eating what you enjoy are going to turn out pretty damn well.

## Myth #10: Wine Is Fattening

A four-ounce glass of white wine contains approximately 104 calories. A four-ounce glass of red wine contains about 6 more calories.

**Bottom Line:** Pour me another glass.

## Myth #11: Experts Know

True or false:

1. Experts know more than you. **T or F**
2. They know so much more that only *they* can truly appreciate wine. **T or F**
3. They know what you like. **T or F**

*Answers:*

1. True. A lot of them know more than me too. So what?
2. False. No way! Wine is a beverage everyone can enjoy and appreciate.
3. False. Only you know what you like. The more confident you become in your taste, the more expert you will become in what you like.

**Bottom Line:** Wine is subjective. Everyone's taste is different. Thus, each and every one of us has the capacity to enjoy and appreciate wine. What counts is what you like and your ability to get it.

# CONCLUSION

Why does wine have to be so hard? Price, pronunciation, experts, cellars, technique, old wines, vintages, scores, and calories. Why can't it be easy? All you want is to do the right thing so you don't embarrass yourself in a restaurant or wineshop. You just want to have fun.

What's holding you back? Is it fear, the unknown, or a lack of confidence in your own taste? Maybe you're not even sure of what you like or have trouble describing what you like. Relax. All wine experts, connoisseurs, or sommeliers started with a first sip. They overcame their fear of wine and embarrassment and kept on sipping, learning as they went along, creating an aroma and taste memory of what they liked.

# TRUE OR FALSE

1.  Expensive is better when it comes to wine. **T or F**
2.  Cheaper is better when it comes to wine. **T or F**
3.  The first step in learning about wine is understanding jargon and correct pronunciation. **T or F**
4.  It is always better to have a big cellar. **T or F**
5.  White wine tastes better ice-cold. **T or F**
6.  Red wine tastes better slightly cool. **T or F**
7.  Beer is easier to open than wine. **T or F**
8.  Wines need to breathe. **T or F**
9.  The British prefer their wines very, very young. **T or F**
10. Old wines do it better. **T or F**
11. Vintage counts in Bordeaux. **T or F**
12. Wine is fattening. **T or F**
13. Only experts can truly understand and enjoy wine. **T or F**

# ANSWERS

1.  False
2.  False
3.  False
4.  A trick question. A big cellar is more fun, but only if you share and drink the wines you have collected. If your big cellar is only for investment purposes, the stock market offers a better return on investment.
5.  False
6.  True
7.  True
8.  False, but if you prefer your wines to breathe before serving, then go right ahead. Taste in wine and certain wine techniques is purely subjective.

9. False

10. False

11. True

12. Another trick question. The caloric content of a glass of wine is, in the scheme of things, small unless you are on a strict diet. For most of us, a glass or two or three of wine a day is not going to significantly increase our waistline.

13. Absolutely and totally false!!!! Wine is a beverage that everyone can understand and enjoy.

# FIRST SIPS

*For Joseph DeLissio, Wine Director for the River Cafe in New York City, his first sip was Boone's Farm Apple Wine: "The vintage was March. A very good month for apple wine." A self-professed "Soave guy" when he first started working at the River Cafe, DeLissio gives a lot of credit to his dog, Jake. "I was twenty-three, a bachelor, and tasting good wine for the first time," he remembers. "I'd take Jake, his dish, and a few bottles to the park. I thought it was the perfect setup—a couple wines and a dog—to meet women. The funny thing is that I couldn't stand Puligny-Montrachet at the time, but Jake loved it. It was the only wine he would drink. And I poured him a taste of every bottle I opened. I wasn't ready for a fine white Burgundy, but my dog was. It made me realize I needed a little education and tasting experience before good wine would make sense for me."*

*Michael Bonadies*

2

# A QUESTION OF TASTE

*"Every night before I go to bed I pray that people with taste get money and people with money get taste."*

**—Overheard in a New York City restaurant**

*"Revenge is a dish best savored cold."*

**—An old Italian saying**

## NO, IT'S NOT A DREAM

*FADE IN:*

INT. MOVIE SET—DAY

*The DIRECTOR, WRITER, STUDIO EXECS, and ACTOR TYPES crowd around a TV monitor.*

*CLOSE IN ON:*

THE TV MONITOR

*AS YOU (that's right, you're the HERO, the star of this big-budget action movie) vanquish the last HENCHMAN and turn to free your CO-STAR, a superstud hunk/gorgeous babe (circle the one that's to your taste). But MR. X, the arch-villain, who you swear is your brother-in-law's exact double, activates the BOMB your CO-STAR is tied to. TENSION BUILDS as the seconds count down and YOU can't decide which wire to cut . . . 10, 9, 8, 7, 6, 5, 4, and you snip.*

MOVIE SET

*AS EVERYONE erupts in applause. The scene is a winner! YOU smile modestly, accepting EVERYONE's raves, and notice your CO-STAR's hand on your thigh.*

CUT TO:

INT. RESTAURANT—NEXT DAY

*Lights, cameras, action—oops. The HERO and the DIRECTOR argue heatedly.*

**HERO**

*(adamant)*

The fate of the world is in my hands and you're trying to tell me I don't know a damn thing about wine.

**DIRECTOR**

But you don't.

**HERO**

My character does.

*The DIRECTOR rolls his eyes as the HERO storms off the set.*

**HERO**

*(looking back)*

Rewrite the scene or I'm not working.

CUT TO:

INT. RESTAURANT—NEXT DAY

*A busy restaurant. Every table is filled as WAITERS hurry about the room delivering food and drinks. The HERO and CO-STAR snuggle at the best table as WAITER #1 (a dead ringer for the wineshop salesperson who couldn't believe you didn't know what Viognier is) places wineglasses on your table as the SOMMELIER (identical to the sommelier who corrected your pronunciation) presents the bottle, wrapped in a napkin hiding the label, with a flourish.*

> **SOMMELIER**
> *(pouring a taste)*
> Compliments of Mr. X.

*MR. X raises his champagne glass to the HERO and CO-STAR in a mock toast.*

> **SOMMELIER**
> Mr. X doesn't believe you can identify this wine.

> **HERO**
> And the wager?

> **SOMMELIER**
> Correctly identify the wine and you'll live to enjoy your dessert. Fail . . .

*SOMMELIER pulls back tuxedo jacket to reveal a large automatic pistol. And a LOOK REVEALS that WAITERS #1 and #2 are armed with knives.*

> **SOMMELIER**
> *(continuing)*
> . . . you won't have to worry about leaving a tip.

*The HERO raises glass in toast to MR. X, accepting the wager. MR. X smiles.*

> **HERO**
> *(to Sommelier)*
> How about a hint?

*SOMMELIER shakes his head.*

THE HERO

*Getting serious, tilts the glass against the white tablecloth, noting that its bright garnet red color indicates a wine of some, but not great, age.*

**HERO**

Less than a decade old.

*The SOMMELIER betrays no reaction. The HERO swirls the glass, releasing the wine's aromas, then sniffs once, twice, and smiles.*

**HERO**

Marvelous.

*(swirls and sniffs again)*

Black cherries and cassis with just a hint of oak.

*(thinks)*

Ah, mint . . . definitely California . . . Cabernet Sauvignon.

But more than just a dollop of Merlot.

*(sniffs again)*

Perhaps a touch of Cabernet Franc too.

*(sniffs again, zeroing in)*

Sonoma for sure.

*A drop of sweat beads on the SOMMELIER's forehead. The HERO is in the zone and CO-STAR is so impressed. The HERO takes another sip as THE TENSION BUILDS.*

**HERO**

Elegant with soft tannins. Wonderfully balanced.

It's drinking perfectly. Delicious . . .

*(to SOMMELIER)*

Would you like a taste?

*The SOMMELIER shakes his head.*

*Michael Bonadies*

(another sip)

I've got it!! The vintage is 1990.

And the winery is—

*Before the HERO can finish, the SOMMELIER pulls his gun. In one motion, the HERO flips the wine into the SOMMELIER's eyes, grabs the bottle, and pushes the CO-STAR down to the floor as BULLETS FLY, hitting just where the wine and CO-STAR sat only moments before. The HERO puts the bottle in a safe spot and flips the table over as WAITER #1 pulls his knife and the ballet of violence begins.*

CUT TO:

THE HERO

*Confronted by WAITER #1's slashing knife, the HERO picks up a corkscrew. One LOOK REVEALS that it is no match for WAITER #1's BIG KNIFE, and the HERO drops it for a BUS BIN FILLED WITH DIRTY PLATES, which the HERO hurls at WAITER #1. THE HERO then flings A ROUND DRINK TRAY like a Frisbee, knocking the gun out of the SOMMELIER's hand as the CO-STAR brains him with the enormous winelist. The HERO bows in CO-STAR's direction and then sidesteps WAITER #1's slashing knife, grabs a full decanter off a table, and smashes the decanter over WAITER #1's head.*

**H**ERO

(to COWERING COUPLE the decanter belonged to)

Sorry.

*The HERO looks up TO SEE WAITER #2 charge with knife drawn. The HERO spins and grabs two heavy silver plate covers off a tray and smashes them together like cymbals, with WAITER #2's head caught in between.*

CUT TO:

MR. X

*Who dabs his lips daintily with a napkin and pulls a machine pistol from under the table.*

THE HERO

*WHO vaults over a banquette as MR. X fires and misses everything but the bottle of wine that started the wager. The bottle shatters, showering the HERO with wine and pieces of glass. The HERO SEES THE LABEL: Jordan Vineyard & Winery Cabernet Sauvignon 1990.*

**HERO**

Yes!!!!

*Hating sore losers, the HERO picks up the SOMMELIER's gun and checks to see if it is loaded. The HERO jumps up ready to fire, ONLY TO SEE THAT:*

*MR. X has taken the CO-STAR hostage and is backing out of the room.*

**MR. X**

Bye-bye.

*The HERO slumps as if in resignation, but it's not. The HERO has simply had enough and FIRES, hitting Mr. X right between the eyes as the CO-STAR screams.*

CUT TO:

THE HERO—MOMENTS LATER

*The HERO lifts Mr. X's bottle of champagne out of its wine bucket, admires it approvingly, grabs two champagne glasses, and walks out arm in arm with the CO-STAR.*

FADE OUT

# THERE'S NO ACCOUNTING FOR TASTE

Wouldn't you just love it to be so easy? A star "tantrum" and—poof—you're a great wine-taster and your wine-snob brother-in-law catches one between the eyes. Unfortunately, in civilized societies like ours, there is a price to pay if you shoot your brother-in-law, no matter how satisfying it would be. And life, as well as the pursuit of wine knowledge, is filled with a few more obstacles than even the most action-packed screenplay. So what's in it for you to keep reading and learning in an effort to become a more able and confident winetaster?

**Short Term**

1. You get to taste more wine. Since most wines taste good, this part is fun.
2. Performance anxiety becomes a thing of the past as your newly acquired powers of perception and articulation enable you to communicate what you see, smell, and taste in a wine.

**Long Term**

1. You get to taste more wine, and since most wines taste good, this part is fun too.
2. You learn what you like and why.
3. Knowing what you like and how to describe it gets you the wine you want more often than not.
4. Adventure and discovery come your way as you confidently explore the world of wine and all it offers.
5. You realize, once and for all, that there is no accounting for taste (however you became related by marriage to this said brother-in-law being a perfect example).

# YOUR TASTE IS KING

*"Taste, the only good taste is your taste . . . if you've got it."*
**—An old New York waiter to a customer**

For better or worse, taste is something everyone has. Yet no two senses of taste are exactly alike. What is taste? Its etymology derives from the Old French word *taste,* meaning "touching" or "touch." And the Oxford English Dictionary defines "taste" as: 1) "a trying, testing; a trial, test, examination"; 2) "the act of tasting, or perceiving the flavor of a thing with the organ of taste"; 3) "of a substance: to have a taste of a specified or implied kind; to produce a certain taste in the mouth; to have a taste or flavor of"; 4) "to produce a particular effect on the mind or feelings; to partake of the nature, character, or quality of."

But what about pink flamingos and velvet paintings of wide-eyed children? Taste is not only a physical act but a psychological and material one as well. We define our individuality, identity, and perceived social standing by how we express our sense of taste through clothing, interior decoration, the car we drive, the music we listen to, and even the wine we drink. A taste for wine presupposes a yearning for greater sophistication and class. As we leave first sips, Jell-O shots, six-packs, and Jägermeister behind, we also tend to distance ourselves from our roots. In the land of opportunity and equality for all, wine and other accoutrements of the good life are signs that we have arrived. Perhaps that is why we often remain insecure in our own taste. No matter how far you've come or have yet to go, the key with wine is to have faith in your own taste. Wine is subjective. What *you* like is what counts. Don't worry if your wife, boyfriend, best friend, or brother-in-law likes something completely different. Your taste is king.

## Your Organ of Taste

"Your organ of taste" sounds risqué, but tasting wine involves your senses and is a very sensual experience. You've got to do it by yourself. Only you smell and taste and perceive what you do. Wine thus makes demands of and rewards all your senses. And being sensual, wine becomes highly subjective. A wine you find delightfully crisp and refreshing your best friend might find lean and sour. Who's right? Who's wrong? No one, but you'd be smart to shy away from your friend's wine recommendations. Here are the steps to becoming a better taster:

1. Learn how to taste wine.
2. Learn how to use all of your senses.
3. Trust all of your senses.
4. Build a vocabulary that enables you to effectively paint a picture of the sensual pleasures a wine offers.

## Your Equipment

Here's a list of the equipment you'll need to taste wine:

1. One bottle of wine, opened
2. One glass, clean
3. Two eyes, focused
4. One nose, not stuffy
5. One tongue, ready
6. Memory and imagination
7. Faith in your own abilities
8. Notebook and pen

If you have all of the above and are able to walk and chew gum at the same time, you're ready to rock and roll.

## But First, Sensual and Other Subversive Pleasures

Tasting wine is about seeking pleasure, pure and simple. And that might just be the problem. This is the country that hanged witches, banned alcohol (and still does in certain towns and counties), even today outlaws various sexual acts, and is preoccupied with catching our leaders and celebrities with their pants down around their ankles. From our Puritanical beginnings to today, we were and still are a people and a nation simultaneously obsessed by, and yet uncomfortable with, anything that gives us pleasure. "No pain, no gain" is probably a more accurate motto for us than "Life, liberty, and the pursuit of happiness." But wine is sensual. It is full of pleasure, tastes great, and makes us happy. Is wine subversive? You bet. In order to taste wine, you have to surrender yourself to its sensual pleasures—the brilliance of its color, its intriguing array of aromas, its layers of flavor and texture, and the emotions and memories it may evoke. So don't be uptight. Relax and enjoy the pleasures that a wine may offer.

## How to Taste Wine

1. Look at it. *What does it look like?*
2. Swirl the wine in the glass to release the aromas, and don't forget to stick your nose in the glass and sniff a few times. *What does it smell like?*
3. Take a slurp, working the wine all over your tongue, letting all of your taste buds have a go at it. *What does it taste like? What does it feel like?*
4. Listen. *What words come to mind to describe your experience of the wine's sensual pleasures?*

5. *Do you like it?*

6. Take notes of your impressions. *Use your imagination, memory, and language skills.*

**Language**

To paint a picture the way you experience a wine's pleasures (or lack thereof), you need words. But which ones? Just think of how you described your last crush to your best friend: "Tall, dark, and handsome, with big sensitive hands, great shoes, and he's got a tattoo . . ." or "Beautiful big eyes and curly hair, and she loves sports and has legs that . . ." Your best friend got the idea right away. In learning to become a better (and more articulate) taster, you want to be able to use language to describe wines you like in a similar way so that the sommelier, server, or salesperson immediately grasps what you might enjoy drinking. "Tall, dark, and handsome" become "rich, full-bodied, and complex." Taste and tell. The bottom line is improving your odds of drinking wines you will enjoy.

# WHAT DOES IT LOOK LIKE?

First of all, hold the wine against a white background and make sure there's enough light. Then look. The first indication of the quality of a wine is the intensity and shade of its color. Green in a white wine indicates youth and acidity. Yellow-gold indicates ripeness or barrel aging. Brown tints in a white mean that it is tired. Purple and blue in red wines indicate youth and richness. Orange or brick notes at the rim of a red speak of age or maturity. With age, white wines gain in color, while reds fade. And let's not forget the glorious stream of bubbles that defines the elegance of a sparkling wine.

Is the wine clear or hazy? If hazy, is it healthy, normal sediment or bacterial spoilage. Your nose will quickly inform you if it is bacterial spoilage. But with the increasing trend toward unfined and unfiltered wines in an effort to produce more intensely flavored wines, there will be more and more bottles in the marketplace that may not be brilliantly clear. There is nothing wrong with these bottles, but if you are accustomed to the clarity of filtered wines, these unfiltered wines may initially provoke suspicion. If you see the words "Unfined" or "Unfiltered" on the label, the winemaker, in an effort to make a more "natural" wine, has decided not to fine (remove solids from the wine with egg whites) or filter (clarify the wine by pumping it through various filter mediums) it because he believes these processes strip wine of aroma and flavor.

## Words to Describe How a Wine Looks:

Brick, brilliant, brown, gold, inky, mahogany, plum, purple, ruby, straw, yellow-gold.

# WHAT DOES IT SMELL LIKE?

The nose knows. While your tongue is able to distinguish only four tastes (sweet, sour, salt, and bitter), your nose is able to distinguish among thousands of aromas. If you don't believe me, try tasting wine with your fingers clamped over your nose or when you have a bad cold. You'll realize that flavor *is* aroma and your nose knows. But what should you smell in a wine?

A wine should smell clean. That means it should not smell like your brother's socks, garlic, or the New Jersey Turnpike. If it smells like vinegar or nail polish, it is spoiled. If it prickles the nose excessively, making you want to sneeze, it has too much sulfur dioxide. If it smells like wet cardboard, it is "corked." (For more on corks and corked wines, see pages 185–86.)

A wine should smell of fruits, flowers, spices, herbs, nuts, oak, and other more specific aromas that are listed on the Wine Aroma Wheel on page 25.

The aroma and bouquet of wine are its most seductive aspects, and the intensity of these smells is part of a wine's level of quality. Aroma is the term for the primary scents from grapes and fermentation in wine. Bouquet refers to the smells that develop with bottle aging and maturity. I find it easier to use the term "nose" to cover both aroma and bouquet, rather than wasting time trying to determine which is which when all the wonderful smells swirl up from the glass. We can see from the Wine Aroma Wheel that the possibilities are endless. What is important is that you grow comfortable identifying and using the descriptors—mint, tea, cherry,

## THE NOSE KNOWS

*You were born with it. Big or small. Aquiline or hooked. As uptight as many of us are—or were—about our noses, we'd be lost without them. How else could we smell danger or a rat?*

*"Smell." Say the word. What comes to mind? Stinky stuff. New York City subways in the summer. Public restrooms. Your brother's socks. Limburger cheese. But say "orange peel" or "gingersnaps" or "charcoal-grilled burgers." What happens? Their smells waft up from the recesses of your memory in a very pleasing fashion.*

etc.—in order to understand and communicate what you smell. As you become a more experienced taster, you will want to develop an awareness of the specific aromas associated with each grape variety. All great wines should express the varietal character of the grape or grapes they are made from.

Smell is the most important sense in evaluating wine, and it is also the most easily fatigued. Sniff in short quick bursts and seek aromas that spark recognition.

## Words to Describe How a Wine Smells:

Apricot, bacon, buttery, cherry, cinnamon, citrus, cola, earthy, mint, smokey, soy, spice, strawberry, tea.

### Stop and Smell the Roses

That's right, stop and smell the roses and violets and honeysuckle and raspberries and strawberries and green apples and pears and lemons and limes and cinnamon and pepper and mushrooms and chocolate too. Rose petal, violet, raspberry, strawberry, cinnamon, pepper, and mushroom may all be found as aromas and flavors in certain red wines. The aromas and flavors of honeysuckle, green apple, pear, lemon, lime, cinnamon, and mushroom can be found in certain white wines. So open your refrigerator, reach for your spice rack, peek in your fruit bowl, and linger in your garden to reacquaint yourself with the majority of aromas and flavors found in wine. The very descriptors that are right on the tip of your tongue are literally right in front of you as you pick a flower, bite into an apple, or squeeze a lemon. Slow down and start paying a little more attention to everyday smells and tastes. You'll be surprised how much better you become at identifying the aromas and flavors in wine.

***How to Use the Wine Aroma Wheel:*** When you sniff the wine, what do you smell? Start at the inner circle of the wheel. Which category does the aroma fall into: FRUITY? HERBACEOUS OR VEGETATIVE? NUTTY? CARAMEL? WOODY? And so on. If FRUITY is your answer, then move to the middle of the wheel and determine if the aroma is: Citrus? Berry? Tree Fruit? Tropical Fruit? Dried Fruit? Or Other? You say Berry. The outer wheel lists blackberry, raspberry, strawberry, and black currant (cassis). It's blackberry! But what if blueberry better describes what you were smelling. Don't worry. The Wine Aroma Wheel is a guide to help *you* describe the aromas you experience when tasting wine. Once you venture into the realm of the outer

# The Wine Aroma Wheel

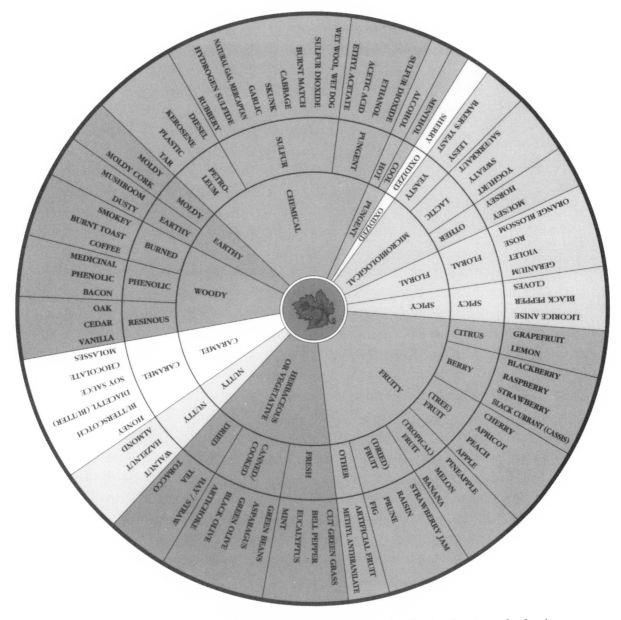

The Wine Aroma Wheel, above (copyright © A. C. Noble 1990), comes in a colored laminated version perfect for when you are tasting or for passing around when you throw a winetasting party. The colored laminated wheel is available from its creator, A. C. Noble, with all profits supporting wine sensory research at the University of California at Davis. Write, call, fax, or e-mail for more information: A. C. Noble, Department of Viticulture and Enology, University of California, One Shields Avenue, Davis, CA 95616. Phone: 530-752-0387. Fax: 530-752-0382. E-mail: acnoble@ucdavis.edu

# Words Used to Describe Wine

| | | | |
|---|---|---|---|
| angular | crass | in-your-face | shy |
| anise | crisp | intense | simple |
| apricot | delicate | lavender | smokey |
| austere | earthy | leather | sour |
| bacon | elegant | light | soy |
| barnyard | enchanting | luscious | spice |
| big | engaging | mahogany | stemmy |
| bitter almond | faded | mellow | straw |
| black olive | fat | melon | strawberry |
| boring | fig | mint | tar |
| brooding | firm | nutty | tart |
| buttery | flabby | peach | tea |
| caramel | flat | pepper | thin |
| cassis | flinty | pineapple | tight |
| cedar | fruity | plain | tired |
| cherry | full | plum | toast |
| cinnamon | gorgeous | prickly | vanilla |
| citrus | green | prune | velvety |
| clove | harsh | purple | violet |
| cloying | heavy | rich | wild |
| clumsy | honeyed | ripe | yellow-gold |
| cola | hot | rough | yummy |
| complex | inky | ruby | |
| concentrated | insipid | seductive | |

wheel and specific aromas, you are talking about thousands of possibilities. The Wine Aroma Wheel has room to list only 87. Most of the aromas you will encounter in tasting wine are familiar, nearly all of them locked up in your memory bank. When you taste, set your mind free. Don't worry about being right or wrong. Simply concentrate on seeking out the words that best express the aromas and flavors you are experiencing in the wine.

*Michael Bonadies*

# DISCOVERING WHITE AND RED WINE AROMAS

*This is a two-part tasting in which the aromas common to white and red wines are examined.*

*The Wine Aroma Wheel, while helpful, does not differentiate among aromas in white and red wines. The varietal profiles that can be found in Chapters 5 and 6 list some of the specific aromas found in white and red wines and are helpful in choosing the aroma essences to be examined.*

### Part 1: White Wine Aromas

*Choose as neutral and characterless a white wine as possible. Add a little of each of the following "aroma essences" to a separate glass of this white wine by mashing, squeezing, grinding, or shredding: almond, apple, apricot, banana, clove, grapefruit, hazelnut, honey, lemon, lime, melon, nutmeg, peach, pear, pineapple, vanilla, etc. Label each glass according to the specific aroma essence represented and place the glasses on a table. Take your time smelling each essence.*

### Part 2: Red Wine Aromas

*Choose as neutral and characterless a red wine as possible. Add a little of each of the following "aroma essences" to a separate glass of this red wine by mashing, squeezing, grinding, or shredding: black olive, black pepper, cassis, cherry, cinnamon, clove, green pepper, mint, mushroom, raspberry, star anise, strawberry, tea, tobacco, vanilla, white pepper, etc. Label each glass according to the specific aroma essence represented and place the glasses on a table. Take your time smelling each essence.*

# WHAT DOES IT TASTE LIKE?

The primary sensor for taste is the tongue. However, the tongue's repertoire is rather crude, as it is able to distinguish only sweet, sour, salt, bitter, and texture (which is really the province of touch).

Sugar in wine is immediately appealing and seductive—our tongue likes it without thinking. But with a little thought and inspection, sugar often becomes too cloying and begins to bore.

Acidity in wine can be refreshing and invigorating. Acidity cleanses the palate, refreshes the appetite, and balances the fruit and richness in a wine. Acidity also contributes to a wine's ability to age gracefully. And acidity in dessert wines acts as an important counterbalance to the wine's sweetness, preventing it from being cloying. However, some tasters may perceive acidity as a fault and view the wine as sour.

Bitter flavors can help balance an otherwise soft and formless wine, but if they are too strong, the wine is poorly made and may not be to your taste.

However, when discussing what a wine tastes like, we do not limit ourselves solely to our tongue's perception of sweet, sour, salt, or bitter. Our nose aids us in perceiving the flavors we taste in a wine, and our mouth helps us experience a wine's texture.

## Words to Describe How a Wine Tastes:

Apricot, bacon, bitter, buttery, cherry, cinnamon, citrus, cola, dry, earthy, mint, smokey, sour, soy, spice, strawberry, sweet, tea. Note that a wine's flavors are often hinted at by its aromas.

# WHAT DOES IT FEEL LIKE?

The tongue and mouth's perception of texture can tell a lot about a wine. Is the wine round or angular, lean or fat, full or thin, light or heavy? If the wine is astringent, it may be a young Cabernet Sauvignon, if supple and sweet, a lush, late-harvest Riesling; if rich and full with a lively acidity, a Chardonnay. An appealing texture is an important component of a wine, and the "weight" of a wine on the tongue is an indication of its relative richness and level of alcohol.

## Words to Describe How a Wine Feels:

Angular, austere, crisp, fat, firm, flabby, full, harsh, heavy, lean, light, luscious, lush, rich, round, sharp, thin, tight, velvety.

# IN TOUCH WITH THE INNER WINE

Tasting a wine also involves determining its personality. What emotions or personality characteristics does your experience of the wine bring to mind? Is the wine forward or shy, seductive or aggressive, enchanting or uptight?

## Words to Describe a Wine's Personality:

Aggressive, brooding, engaging, exotic, mellow, mysterious, seductive, shy, straightforward, reticent.

# YUCK OR YUM—LASTING IMPRESSIONS

You look, you swirl, you sniff, and you taste. Are the aromas focused and intriguing? Does the wine taste like what it smelled like? What is its finish like—do the flavors linger in your mouth, or do they disappear after a short burst of intensity? The oral impression of the wine should be clean, and the intensity and complexity of flavor an indication of its quality. In addition to the flavors, you should also consider the balance of alcohol, tannin, sugar, and acidity in the wine. Does the wine give the sensation of these components being balanced? Or does one or more stand out and draw attention to itself? Balance is ultimately what you look for when you taste. If all the elements of a wine are in balance and harmony and thus pleasurable, all you have to ask yourself is, Did I like it?

## SPITTING

*If you are tasting a number of wines at one sitting—SPIT! Why? Because as you taste and swallow, alcohol enters your bloodstream and begins to dull your senses. Alcohol relaxes you, but it also lessens your ability to concentrate and to perceive the sensory stimuli the wines are sending your way. If you want to learn, don't forget to spit. But make note of the wines you like so that you can go back and enjoy them after the tasting is finished.*

### How to Spit
*While I have seen experienced tasters hit a spit bucket from 6 feet away, I don't recommend it unless you can get your dry cleaning done for free. For a wine tasting, you will need Styrofoam cups and a bucket. Place a Styrofoam cup in front of each taster, as well as a glass of water (water helps refresh the palate) and paper towels. Place the bucket on the table. Taste and spit discreetly into the cup. As it fills, dump the contents into the bucket.*

## TAKING NOTES ON YOUR IMPRESSIONS

Once the words start to come—and they will come—write them down! This is where a notebook comes in handy. Allow one page per wine. Set up the page as follows:

**PRODUCER:** *Chalk Hill*

**NAME OF WINE** *Chardonnay*

**VINTAGE** *1994*

**APPEARANCE:** *clear, rich gold color*

**NOSE:** *opulent scents of nutmeg, pear, lime and spice with hints of vanilla*

**FLAVORS:** *apple, pear, roasted nuts, spice and an endless lemon-lime finish*

**TEXTURE:** *rich, round and lush—balanced with a lively acidity, elegant and graceful*

**PUT IT ALL TOGETHER:** *A rich, well-balanced Chardonnay with concentrated aromas & flavors and a refreshing acidity.*

**YUCK OR YUM?** *Definitely Yum!*

**PRODUCER:** *Joseph Phelps Vineyards*

**NAME OF WINE** *Insignia*

**VINTAGE** *1992 (67% Cabernet Sauvignon, 33% Merlot)*

**APPEARANCE:** *clear, brilliant ruby color*

**NOSE:** *bright and focused: layers of cassis, mint, spice, chocolate; hints of vanilla and cedar*

**FLAVORS:** *layered and complex sweet fruit: cassis, spice, mint & chocolate; very concentrated*

**TEXTURE:** *Dense and concentrated with a powerful richness balanced by firm tannins and a bright acidity*

**PUT IT ALL TOGETHER:** *Lots going on, tons of aroma and flavor, rich and powerful but still balanced and elegant.*

**YUCK OR YUM?** *It's a Yum!*

Appearance, nose (aroma and bouquet), and flavors are self-explanatory. Texture is the sensation a wine creates in your mouth—is it soft or hard, tannic or smooth, lush or tight, light or full-bodied, and does it have a long or short finish? Now that you have broken the wine into pieces according to each sense, put it back together in your own words. Paint those sensual pleasures vividly and the wine will have a distinct personality. Don't be afraid to take your time. Take another sniff, another sip, another look if you need to. Make it fun, always remembering that "yuck" or "yum" is strictly personal.

# TASTING TIPS

1. It's better to taste and take your notes before your guests arrive, to avoid looking geeky.

2. Tasting parties are fun. Theme them:
   - Chardonnays From Around the World.
   - Showdown: California Pinot Noir versus Oregon Pinot Noir.
   - Bang for Your Buck: white or red, nothing over $10.
   - New World vs. Old: California Cabernet Sauvignon versus Bordeaux.
   - Trivia Quiz: Pick a vintage to taste and then research the sports, fashion, history, politics, and other trivia questions from that year. Play the music from that year as you taste.

# CONCLUSION

Practice. Taste and taste some more. Keep a notebook and record your impressions. Buy several good wine books, such as Hugh Johnson's *The World Atlas of Wine,* Jancis Robinson's *The Oxford Companion to Wine,* and James Halliday's *Wine Atlas of California.* Look up and read about every wine you taste, but only after you've tasted it. Don't let an encyclopedia or a wine magazine's description unduly influence your expectations of a wine. Taste it for yourself and decide whether or not you like it. After reading about a wine, look up any references that are appropriate. For example, you've just tasted Joseph Phelps's Napa Valley Cabernet Sauvignon. While this specific wine is probably not listed, Joseph Phelps Vineyards should be. Look it up. Then look up Napa Valley, Cabernet Sauvignon, and any other references or terms that spark your curiosity.

*Michael Bonadies*

The next time you enjoy a bottle of wine in a restaurant or at a friend's house, write down the name and producer. Look them up in your encyclopedia. Before you know it, you will be a more confident and knowledgeable taster and consumer.

The great thing about wine is that you never stop learning. The only way to stop learning is to stop tasting. Not only are new wineries and new wines sprouting up all over the world, but every vintage brings new wines to taste and explore. As you explore, you may find that your taste changes. The typical taste arc for most American wine fans is as follows:

1. The exploration begins with a sweet, soda-pop-like wine, such as Boone's Farm, White Zinfandel, or sangria, and moves on to white wine, primarily Chardonnay and Sauvignon Blanc, with detours to discover Chenin Blanc, Riesling, Viognier, and Gewürztraminer.

2. Next is a leap into the land of reds. The first curious sips are of Cabernet Sauvignon– or Merlot–based wines. These sips may lead to experimentation with Italian reds, Rhône varietals, and Zinfandel.

3. Then, with the Holy Grail in sight (whether the individual fan knows it or not), sparkling, dessert, and fortified wines are given a try.

4. At the end of the journey lies the Holy Grail: Pinot Noir. Pinot Noir is perhaps the most difficult grape to grow and vinify but produces the most incredibly delicious, mysterious, and seductively hedonistic wines going.

As you taste and explore, you may find that while you have tried reds, you are a white wine drinker; or if you've discovered the joys of red, then Merlot is for you. That's okay. The goal is to discover what you like.

# WARNING!!!!

*Have you ever said, "Wow, is that red tannic, ouch!" or "Errrrr, boy, is that white sharp and acidic!"? Wine was meant to be drunk with food. The "painful" experience of tannins and acidity greatly lessens once you start eating. So don't dismiss a wine that isn't immediately and totally pleasing. Give it a chance with food.*

# PRACTICE TASTING

Using the tasting format below, taste a white and red wine you like.

**PRODUCER:** _____

**NAME OF WINE** _____

**VINTAGE** _____

**APPEARANCE:** _____

_____

_____

_____

**NOSE:** _____

_____

_____

**FLAVORS:** _____

_____

_____

**TEXTURE:** _____

_____

_____

**PUT IT ALL TOGETHER:** _____

_____

_____

**YUCK OR YUM?** _____

_____

_____

_____

_____

**PRODUCER:** _____

**NAME OF WINE** _____

**VINTAGE** _____

**APPEARANCE:** _____

_____

_____

**NOSE:** _____

_____

_____

**FLAVORS:** _____

_____

_____

**TEXTURE:** _____

_____

_____

**PUT IT ALL TOGETHER:** _____

_____

_____

**YUCK OR YUM?** _____

_____

_____

_____

_____

_____

_____

# QUESTIONS

1. What is the most important sense in tasting wine? _____

2. List the steps involved in tasting wine:

    a) look

    b) swirl

    c) _____

    d) _____

    e) _____

    f) _____

3. What does a yellow-gold color in a white wine indicate?

    a) Barrel aging or _____

    A green color in a white wine?

    b) _____

    Brown?

    c) _____

4. Haziness in wine can indicate (two of the below):

    a) bacterial spoilage

    b) disintegration of the cork

    c) an unfiltered or unfined wine, a new trend

    d) tannins

5. A sure sign of bacterial spoilage is: _____

    a) a foul smell

    b) a wet and crumbly cork

    c) sediment in the bottle

    d) all of the above

6. What do wines need? _____

7. True or false: Knowing how to describe what you like in a wine will help get you the wine you will enjoy more often than not. _____**T or F**

8. Which of the following words can be used to describe a wine?

    a) seductive

    b) big

    c) plum

    d) ruby

e) violet

f) all of the above

9. Define a wine's aroma: _____

10. Define a wine's bouquet:_____

11. Define a wine's nose:_____

12. Your tongue is able to distinguish:

a) sweet

b) _____

c) _____

d) _____

13. A wine is considered to be in balance if its alcohol, tannin, sugar, and acidity are perceived to be in harmony. **T or F**

14. List words that describe textures in wine:

a) angular

b) _____

c) _____

d) _____

e) _____, etc.

15. Using your own words, describe your favorite wine: _____

_____

_____

_____

_____

_____

16. True or false: Your taste is king. _____**T or F**

# ANSWERS

1. Smell

2. 

c) sniff

d) slurp

e) perceive the pleasures (or lack thereof)

f) take notes

**3.**

    a)  ripeness

    b)  youth and acidity

    c)  tired

**4.** a or c

**5.** a

**6.** Food

**7.** True

**8.** f

**9.** The fruit-based smells in a wine

**10.** The smells in wine that develop with bottle aging

**11.** The term that encompasses both aroma and bouquet

**12.**

    b)  sour

    c)  salt

    d)  bitter

**13.** True

**14.**

    b)  full

    c)  heavy

    d)  lean

    e)  lush

    f)  round

    g)  sharp

    h)  thin, etc.

**15.** Whatever words you use are right.

**16.** True

*Michael Bonadies*

# | 3 |

# THE BASICS

You're a famous movie star and your last picture was a huge hit. It grossed over $500 million worldwide and you've just inked a three-picture deal for $24 million per. You most definitely have the basics covered. But this wine thing's getting you hooked. You want to know more. For example, what's oak got to do with it?

## WINE

Wine, vino, or righteous juice—whatever you want to call it, it's the finished product, the beverage this book is all about, so let's start there.

**What is wine?**
Fermented grape juice.

**What is fermentation?**
Fermentation occurs when yeast converts the sugar in ripe grapes into alcohol, carbon dioxide, and heat.

**What is yeast?**
A single-celled organism that loves sugar and is essential to the production of wine.

**What is wild yeast?**
A single-celled organism that loves to party. Not. Actually, wild (or native) yeast is an air-

borne microorganism that exists in the vineyard and winery and sparks spontaneous fermentation. And since many California winemakers don't want anything spontaneous happening with their grapes, sulfur dioxide is added to kill this yeast.

### What is cultured yeast?

A philosophy major. Almost. Cultured yeast is a single strain of laboratory-bred yeast with highly predictable fermentation behaviors and flavor characteristics. In other words, more of a sure thing as opposed to the riskier wild yeast.

### Why are red wines red?

Red wines are red because fermentation extracts color from the grape skins. White wines are not fermented with the skins present.

### What types of grapes are used?

Any ripe grape can be made into wine. But only certain grape varieties belonging to the genus *Vitis vinifera* produce what are considered fine wines.

### What is *Vitis vinifera*?

The genus of grape vines of European origin—Chardonnay, Sauvignon Blanc, Riesling, Cabernet Sauvignon, Merlot, Pinot Noir, and Syrah, to mention a few—that constitute the most significant commercial varieties cultivated around the world today.

### What is *Vitis labrusca*?

The genus of grape vines native to North America. They are not in the same class as the *vinifera* wines because of their "foxy" aromas and flavors. However, they are important because of their resistance to the vine pest phylloxera.

### What is a varietal wine?

A varietal wine is a wine bottled from predominantly one grape variety and labeled as such. The most popular varietal wines in the United States today are Chardonnay, Cabernet Sauvignon, and Merlot.

### What is a sparkling wine?

A wine with bubbles.

## What is a fortified wine?

A wine to which brandy or a neutral spirit is added to produce a wine with higher alcohol content. Port, Madeira, and sherry are fortified wines.

## What is aroma?

The primary scents from grapes and fermentation.

## What is bouquet?

The more complex smells that are produced by bottle aging.

## What is a wine's nose?

A way to talk about what a wine really smells like without getting hung up on exactly what an aroma is as opposed to what a bouquet is.

## What is "oaky"?

The term used to describe wine with aromas and flavors influenced by oak, usually through fermentation and/or aging in oak barrels. Because of the expense of oak barrels, lower-priced wines may have had oak chips added prior to fermentation in an attempt to attain a similar "oakiness."

## What aromas and flavors does fermentation and/or aging in oak impart to a wine?

Butterscotch, smokey, toast, and vanilla, to mention a few.

## Does the fermentation or aging of a wine in stainless-steel tanks impart a "steely" flavor or aroma?

No. Stainless-steel tanks are neutral vessels that preserve the straightforward fruit aromas and flavors of a wine. The descriptor "steely" is most frequently associated with cold-climate Chardonnays, particularly those from the Chablis region of France.

## What are tannins?

Tannins are compounds that pucker your mouth with a noticeable drying effect in very strong tea and certain red wines. They are extracted from the skins, stems, and seeds of grapes as well as from the wooden barrels that some wines are aged in. Tannins help red wines age because of their antioxidant properties. With age, tannins usually become less noticeable. Tannins also become much less noticeable when a red wine is drunk with food. Hence, the saying "What this wine needs is a big steak."

**Why are tannins less noticeable in older reds?**
In young reds, tannins are relatively short or small molecules that produce a drying or puckering effect in the mouth. As wine ages, tannin molecules link up and form chains that have less of a drying effect. Eventually, with sufficient age, a large percentage of a wine's tannins fall out of the wine as sediment. In recent years, winemakers have learned how to make young reds more approachable by creating larger and softer tannins.

**What is acidity?**
Several different acids occur naturally in grapes. As the grapes mature and ripen, acidity levels often fall off as sugar levels rise. (Ever notice how sour an unripened grape tastes? That's acidity.) If the grapes are harvested when the acidity and sugar are in balance, a balanced wine results. Acidity tends to be more noticeable in whites.

**What is acetic acid?**
Vinegar, baby.

**What is body?**
The weight of a wine in your mouth. Is it light, medium, or full-bodied?

**What is texture?**
The feel of a wine in your mouth plus the weight of its body. Is it lush or tight, round or sharp, rich or austere?

**What is concentration?**
The relative intensity of a wine's aroma and flavors. Typically, the more concentrated a wine is, the more intensely focused are the aromas and flavors it offers. Concentration is a reflection of vintage, as better vintages deliver riper, better-balanced, more intensely flavored grapes, which produce wines with greater concentration.

## What is complexity?

Layers and layers of sensual pleasure. The more complex a wine, the more it reveals in terms of smell, taste, and texture.

## What is length?

The persistence of a wine's flavor and texture in your mouth. Also known as a wine's finish. With a short finish, the flavors vanish in mid-sip, with a long finish, the flavors linger, inviting another sip.

## What is balance?

When a wine tastes seamless because all its major elements—fruit, sugar, acidity, tannin, and alcohol—are in harmony. Balance is an important indicator of a wine's quality.

## Why are California wines named differently from French wines?

Marketing.

## Why?

In France, wines are named after their geographic location—for example, Chassagne-Montrachet "Morgeot," which tells you the wine is from the Morgeot vineyard in the village of Chassagne-Montrachet. But that's all gibberish unless you know that it is a white wine made from Chardonnay grapes in the Côte de Beaune region of Burgundy. In order to distinguish itself from France and from generic jug wines labeled Chablis, Burgundy, and Claret, California producers decided to name their more ambitious wines after the different grape varieties from which they were made. Today, if a label reads Chardonnay, by law it must contain at least 75% Chardonnay grapes. Geographic labeling makes sense in France, where the vineyards have proven themselves over thousands of years. California doesn't have that history or track record. Specific regions and vineyards have just recently begun to consistently produce wines that attract consumer attention. And isn't Chardonnay a lot easier to pronounce than Chassange-Montrachet "Morgeot."

# The Exception: Insignia

*Meritage or proprietary wines are the exception to the labeling law requiring 75% or more of a single variety. If your wine's final blend is only 70% Cabernet Sauvignon, what do you put on the label? "Almost Cabernet"? It wouldn't sell and the BATF (Bureau of Alcohol, Tobacco, and Firearms) would never approve the label. The solution is to give a name to your "Almost Cabernet"—a proprietary name.*

*Joseph Phelps Vineyards Insignia 1974 was the first California proprietary wine. The term "Meritage," which is employed to represent the category of Bordeaux-style proprietary wines, was not coined until years later. "Insignia" was born during Phelps's first harvest. Eight barrels of Cabernet Sauvignon and Merlot were found to be exceptional. Joe Phelps didn't want to blend them into his Napa Valley Cabernet Sauvignon. And since he disliked the term "Reserve," which doesn't mean anything legally, the only solution was to invent his own name for this special wine—Insignia.*

*From this almost accidental beginning, and a blend of 94% Cabernet Sauvignon and 6% Merlot, Insignia has evolved with the stated goal of representing the highest expression of winemaking possible in any given vintage with Napa Valley grapes. Over the years, this blend of Bordeaux varietals (Cabernet Sauvignon, Merlot, and Cabernet Franc) has seen as much as 94% and as little as 14% Cabernet Sauvignon, with the average varying between 50% and 70%.*

*Proprietary wines are an increasingly popular category. Imagination is the only limitation for these blends and their names. While the majority are blends of red Bordeaux varieties, there is a growing trend toward white blends as well. Other proprietary wines worth checking out include Cain Five, Conundrum, Dominus, Opus One, Rubicon, and Viader.*

# THE VINEYARD

The vineyard is where the action is today, as the ravages of phylloxera present new opportunities and California winemakers realize that future improvements in wine quality will come as the result of hard work and viticultural advances.

**What is a vineyard?**

A vineyard is where grapes grow.

## What is viticulture?

The agricultural science of growing grape vines.

## Why are some vineyards better than others?

A great vineyard is the sweet spot where all the elements and variables of nature come together to produce great grapes. Great grapes make great wines. The better the vineyard, the better the grapes and the better the wine.

## Does it matter which grape is planted in a vineyard?

Very much so. The grape variety must be matched to the vineyard's soil and climate in order for it to excel in that vineyard.

## What part does climate play?

The climatic conditions that are unique to a vineyard—temperature, rainfall, humidity, wind, exposure to the sun—constitute the microclimate of a vineyard. These factors, especially temperature, determine the appropriateness of a specific grape variety for that vineyard site.

## What part does soil play?

The soil provides the nutrients and water necessary for the growth of the vine.

## What is *terroir?*

A French term that encompasses the entire ecology of a vineyard. It is often incorrectly used as another word for a vineyard's soil. This is because in France the soil's characteristics and its effect on the wine are viewed as most important, while in California the emphasis has always been on climate.

## What is an Approved Viticultural Area?

An area recognized as a premier winegrowing area. While California decided to name its wines after grapes, it increasingly recognizes the importance of place—that is, some regions and vineyards produce better wine than others. What this means to the consumer is that, more often than not, the more specific the label is in listing region and vineyard, the better the wine will be. In the United States, a region can be recognized by law as an Approved Viticultural Area (AVA) if it shows evidence of similar growing conditions throughout the region and historic usage of the proposed name. Current AVAs include Napa Valley, with its sub-AVAs of Atlas Peak, Howell Mountain, Mount Veeder, Oakville, Rutherford, Spring Mountain, and Stag's Leap District. Other AVAs include Alexander Valley, Carneros, Edna Valley, Mount Harlan, Paso Robles, Russian River Valley, Santa Maria Valley, Santa Ynez Valley, Sonoma Coast, Sonoma Valley, to list just a few. For a winery to put an AVA on its label, the law requires that at least 85% of grapes used to make the wine be from that specific AVA and that at least 75% of the grape variety on the label (i.e., Cabernet Sauvignon) be from that specific AVA.

## What other elements come into play in a vineyard?

Rootstocks, clones, yield, and canopy management. But let's start first with phylloxera.

## What is phylloxera?

Phylloxera is a plant louse (small insect) native to the Eastern United States that kills grape vines by attacking their roots. In the second half of the nineteenth century, phylloxera was inadvertently introduced into Europe, where it came close to destroying all the vineyards, munching its way from country to country. Soon after, it hitchhiked its way on Eastern grape vines to California, where it caused similar devastation.

## What halted the spread of phylloxera?

Native American rootstocks. If you remember your history, back around A.D. 1000, Leif Ericsson "discovered" America and named it Vinland for all the grape vines he found growing there. Native American grape vines grew then and today in spite of phylloxera. Phylloxera doesn't faze them. But they make lousy wine. The solution was to plant their phylloxera–resistant rootstocks in the vineyards and then graft the noble *Vitis vinifera* varieties to those rootstocks. Today, all over Europe and in the United States, Chardonnay, Merlot, Pinot Noir, etc., grow and thrive on native American rootstocks.

## What is the status of phylloxera today?

It hasn't disappeared or given up. It has recently resurfaced as a major problem in California, chewing its way through vineyards and attacking rootstocks that were not as resistant as everyone had believed (specifically, one called AxR #1, which had been very widely planted). This tragedy does have a silver lining. While it is very expensive and heartbreaking to tear up and replant a vineyard destroyed by phylloxera, it also offers the opportunity, in many instances, for California growers to replant a more appropriate grape variety in the vineyard.

### What are rootstocks?

The root sections of American vines or hybrids onto which *Vitis vinifera* vines are grafted in order to defeat phylloxera. Rootstocks are also chosen according to their vigor, drought tolerance, and soil compatibility.

### What are clones?

Clones, in grapespeak, are subvarieties of the same grape that differ from one another in important ways: aroma, flavor, yield, resistance to disease, compatibility with specific rootstocks, etc. Careful clonal selection enables growers to plant the clones that will produce, for example, the best possible Cabernet Sauvignon in a specific vineyard.

### What are old clones?

A marketing term without much meaning.

### What are old vines?

Another marketing term, most frequently applied to old Zinfandel vines. There is no legal definition of what constitutes old, but generally vines do not begin to produce quality grapes until after their fourth or fifth vintage, then decline in production sometime after hitting their twentieth, becoming uneconomic after their fiftieth. Most of the old vine Zinfandel vineyards in question are well over fifty years old, with a number having produced wine for over a hundred years. Is old really better, or have these vines survived all these years because they were planted in exactly the ideal spot for them to succeed? No one really knows for sure, but these old vineyards keep on producing delicious Zinfandels.

### What are vineyard blocks?

Individual sections of a vineyard considered unique because of their specific soil, microclimate, and varietal or clonal selection.

### What is spacing?

How close the vines are planted in a vineyard within a row and between rows.

# THE VINEYARD

*A great vineyard firmly locates one in time and place. It is possible to step out of the car and stroll through the vines, noticing the spacing of the vines, the composition of the soil, and how the morning fog lingers or the late-day sun provides a final burst of warmth. If you're lucky and harvest is near, you can pluck a grape or two, sneaking a taste of what the vintage will be like. The grapes are delicious, full of flavor and memories of vintages past, of bottles shared and enjoyed. The specific aromas and flavors, faded with time, revive with each ripe, lush grape. Suddenly, as you look across the rows of vines, you realize that all those wonderful wines began in the exact place where you stand.*

## What is canopy management?

Canopy management is a fancy term for farming grapes. In spite of all the sophistication and romance surrounding wine, it comes down to tending the soil and growing fruit. The canopy is the foliage, or leaves, of a grape vine. The leaves take sunlight and use its energy to convert carbon dioxide and water into sugar, some of which is then dispatched to the growing grapes. The goal of canopy management is to arrange the leaves through pruning and trellising to achieve a balance in the vine that produces the best fruit possible.

## What is pruning?

Every winter, vineyard workers prune back the vines so that, when the growing season arrives, they produce an optimum number of grape clusters.

## What is trellising?

Grape vines are just that—vines. They want to grow every which way. Trellising is the training of the vines so that they grow in a manner that will achieve the grower's goal: either the best fruit possible or the most fruit possible. While there are many different methods of trellising, most of them use a structure, or trellis, that the vine is trained to grow along so that the foliage will be open and the grape bunches will receive the right amount of sun.

**What is a vintage?**

The growing season, or year, that produces a wine.

**What is the harvest?**

Both the process and time period in which grapes are picked.

**What is the yearly cycle of the vine in California?**

*Winter:* *Pruning*—this is done from November to February, when the vine is dormant. Extremely cold weather can kill the vine.

*Spring:* *Bud break*—the buds of the vine begin to grow in March. Frost is the danger. *Bloom and set*—the grape vine flowers and self-pollinates, setting the stage for the grapes. This occurs in May. Bad weather—cold, rain, wind—can prevent the vines from flowering and the grapes from setting.

*Summer:* The grapes grow. Hail and fungal diseases are the dangers. *Veraison*—the coloring of the grapes—begins in August as the grapes start to ripen.

*Autumn:* Harvest nears. The grapes are closely watched until they are determined to be fully ripe, and then they are harvested. Rain at harvest time is a total bummer.

**When are grapes fully ripe?**

When the sugars and acids reach the desired degree (measured analytically) of ripeness. The goal is to harvest grapes at their peak of ripeness. But ripeness is a relative term. The degree of "ripeness" varies depending on the grape variety and the style of wine to be made. For example, grapes intended for the production of sparkling wine are picked at a lower sugar level and a higher acid level than grapes that will be made into table wines.

**What is yield?**

The total grape crop of a vineyard as measured in tons per acre or pounds per vine.

**What is low yield?**

The fact that a vineyard has produced a small crop, but more important, the current belief that a smaller yield per acre will produce better grapes and thus better wine. While there appears to be some truth to this belief, a low yield, relatively speaking, can vary greatly from variety to variety, vineyard to vineyard, region to region, vintage to vintage.

## What is selection?

Selection is an ongoing process that begins with farming practices in the vineyard, continues with division of the vineyard into blocks, and reaches its peak during harvest. A strict selection is crucial during the harvest in vintages plagued by rain, rot, or uneven ripening, with only the ripest, healthiest grapes vinified and the rest discarded.

## What is a field blend?

It was the old way of doing things in California: planting several varieties in a vineyard so as not to have all your eggs in one basket when it came to the vagaries of weather and vintage. The different varieties were harvested and vinified together to make a single wine.

## Who are the bad guys, other than phylloxera?

*Weather:* Weather is very much a Jekyll-and-Hyde thing when it comes to growing grapes. With great weather, you have a great vintage. Frost, too much rain or not enough rain, hail, wind, cold, heat occurring at the wrong time during a vine's life cycle, can wreak havoc on the quality of the grapes.

*Insects:* In addition to phylloxera, there is the sharpshooter leafhopper, which spreads the deadly Pierce's disease, as well as countless other bugs that feed on grape vines, weakening them and lowering the quality of fruit they are able to produce.

*Fungi, viruses, and other creepy little things:* Virus infections such as fan leaf and leaf roll can weaken and kill the vine. But fungi are a more severe problem year in and year out. Downy mildew and oidium (powdery mildew), black rot and *Botrytis cinerea* (rot) can wipe out an entire vintage and ruin a vineyard.

*Animals:* These include birds, wild pigs, and even humans. If every tourist who came through Napa Valley helped himself to a bunch of ripe grapes, there would be less wine being made.

## Who are the good guys?

*Weather:* The warm days, cool nights, and limited rainfall of California's premier wine-growing regions help produce consistently superior vintages.

*Philosophy:* A change in philosophy in recent years has focused greater attention on the vineyard and farming practices, resulting in innovations that have produced better wines.

*Stress:* A little bit of stress works wonders in producing higher-quality grapes. For vines, it is a matter of a moderate degree of stress involving soil fertility and the availability of water.

In fertile soil and with plenty of water, vines live large and put their energy into growing leaves while neglecting their grapes. In a vineyard with not-so-fertile soil and just enough water to stress the vines, reproductive anxiety sets in and they channel their energy into growing grapes. The result is riper, more flavorful grapes. However, too much stress is just as bad for vines as it is for us.

*Vineyard workers:* The men and women who do the farming, striving to grow the best possible grapes.

# THE WINERY

A simple garage or a palace of technology, the winery is where a year's work in the vineyard comes together in a short, intense burst of energy and effort to transform grapes into wine.

## What is a winery?

A winery is where the grapes are brought after being harvested. It is where the wine is made, aged, and bottled. And during the crush, or harvest, it is often a place where a significant quantity of cold beer is consumed. Wine writers rate vintages with numbers. California cellar rats (winery workers) rate vintages according to the number of cases of beer consumed during the crush.

## What is the crush?

Crush is another name for harvest and incorporates not only the harvesting of the grapes but also their initial processing at the winery.

## Who is a winemaker?

The person who makes the wine. In a large winery, the winemaker may oversee many assistants. In a small winery, the owner is often also the winemaker.

## Who is a winegrower?

A winemaker with a new business card. The term "grower" applies to someone who owns a vineyard, grows the grapes, and then sells them to someone who makes them into wine. A winegrower is a born-again winemaker who not only has changed the title on his business card but praises the glory of the vineyard while keeping real quiet about the neat

# HARVEST

*Following are Oded Shakked's reflections on the days leading up to the harvesting of the grapes he will make into "J," Jordan Sparkling Wine:*

*"During the crucial weeks before harvest, I follow the various vineyards and vineyard blocks very closely, building a mental map of the various flavors that are being developed by the interaction of soil, weather, and plant status. The decision to harvest a particular block occurs only when the flavor profile as well as the analytical data fit within the window that matches the style of wine we are crafting. I view every lot as a unique component and thus may try to maximize a floral aroma from one block while trying to retain a crisp acidity from another. I may choose to leave some Chardonnay on the vine longer to develop greater length in the mid-palate or pick another slightly earlier to prevent the development of "Muscat-y" aromas or bitter phenolic flavors. Just like anyone who enjoys cooking, I tend to be very particular and finicky about my raw ingredients. I can't help, as harvest nears, to taste the grapes from each block before giving the order to start picking."*

equipment he has back at the winery. Winegrowers wear the mantle of modesty and are great for humble quotes like "Wine is made in the vineyard" or "Grow me great grapes and then it's just up to me to not screw them up in the winery."

**What follows are some of the basic winemaking terms that will be used in subsequent discussions of the vinification of white, red, sparkling, and dessert wines. Don't worry about memorizing them. Read through them and refer back to them as needed.**

*Selection:* A process that continues in the winery through fermentation and aging, as tanks, lots, and individual barrels are monitored for quality, with the best ones selected for the final blend.

*Sulfur:* Wine's antibiotic, antifungal, and preservative. While sulfur is used primarily in the winery to prevent oxidation, kill unwanted yeast and bacteria, and disinfect barrels, sulfur dust is applied in the vineyard to prevent the spread of powdery mildew.

*Sulfites:* The various forms of sulfur that may be in wine, some of which are a natural by-product of fermentation. Every wine bottle sold in the United States carries the warning "Contains Sulfites."

*Oxidation:*  The chemical reaction of oxygen with another substance. For example, oxidation is what causes a cut piece of fruit to turn brown and deteriorate. While limited and controlled exposure to the air may be employed during winemaking, for the most part the grapes, the must, and the wine are protected from the harmful effects of oxidation.

*Stemmer-crusher:*  A machine that removes the grapes from their stems, gently crushes the grapes, and creates the must.

*Must:*  The name for the mass of grape juice and pulp resulting from the crushing of grapes. It is the term used in the winery until fermentation is complete and the grapes have become wine.

*Press:*  A machine that presses juice from the must.

*Free-run juice:*  The juice produced by the initial crushing and the first gentle pressings. The good stuff.

*Press juice:*  The juice from subsequent pressings. Higher in acid and tannin (and other bitter compounds) than free-run juice. A proportion of the press juice may be blended back into the free-run juice or sold off separately, depending on its quality and the style of wine desired.

*Stainless-steel fermentation:*  Fermentation of wine in large temperature-controlled stainless-steel tanks.

*Barrel-fermented:*  Said of wine fermented in small, usually oak casks as opposed to larger stainless-steel tanks.

*Oak:*  Think of oak as a spice used by winemakers to attain certain flavors and textures in wine as the result of its being fermented and/or aged in oak barrels. The degree of oak's influence on a wine is determined by:

- the age of the barrel; new barrels impart greater flavor and texture.
- the toast, or char, of the barrel; the insides of the barrels are charred with fire according to the winemaker's specifications—light, medium, or heavy. The heavier the char, the stronger the flavor.
- American or French oak; each imparts different flavors and texture to a wine.
- the particular forest from which the oak has been harvested.

*Carbonic maceration:*  Fermentation that takes place inside of whole, uncrushed grapes, resulting in a fruity wine. Often used in the production of Beaujolais.

*Maceration:* What occurs during the fermentation of red wine when color, flavor, tannin, and aroma are extracted from the grape skins, pulp, and seeds.

*Extended maceration:* What occurs when the skins are allowed to remain in the red wine after fermentation is complete. The goal is to achieve greater extraction of color, aroma, and flavor, as well as a softer, more approachable wine. Seemingly contradictory, extended maceration encourages the development of longer, softer tannins when the grape skins are fully ripe.

*Malolactic fermentation:* A natural, secondary fermentation in wine, following the alcoholic fermentation, in which bacteria converts malic acid (the acid in tart apples) to lactic acid (the acid in milk). This fermentation changes the impression of acidity in a wine by making it taste "softer" while increasing the wine's flavor complexity. The descriptor "buttery" is closely associated with malolactic fermentation (diacetyl, a by-product of malolactic fermentation, is also found in butter). Malolactic fermentation is encouraged in most full-bodied reds and many Chardonnays. Winemakers often will prevent malolactic fermentation in whites like Riesling, Sauvignon Blanc, and Chenin Blanc to retain their crisp acidity.

*Acidification:* The attempt to balance a wine through the addition of tartaric or citric acid. This practice is more common in warm-weather regions like California, where a hot spell can cause the grapes to ripen too rapidly, with a resulting loss of natural acidity. Sufficient acidity is required to help preserve a wine as well as to make it taste fresh and refreshing.

*Chaptalization:* The attempt to balance a wine through the addition of sugar before or during fermentation in order to boost a wine's final alcohol content. If acid is needed in warm regions, then sugar is required in cooler regions when the grapes struggle to ripen and produce sufficient sugar. Alcohol is important to wine not only because it is one of the reasons we make and drink it but also because it helps to stabilize and preserve a wine.

*Residual sugar:* Sugar that remains in the wine after fermentation is complete. Residual sugar is very important for dessert wines.

*Lees:* Dead yeast cells and other solids that fall to the bottom of the fermenting or aging container.

*Lees contact:* After fermentation, leaving the wine on the lees in order to encourage malolactic fermentation and to extract greater flavor and complexity. Lees contact, also known as *sur lie* aging, adds roundness and creaminess to the wine's texture.

*Sediment:* A more commonly used word for the lees. Racking, fining, and filtering remove the sediment with varying degrees of efficiency.

*Clarification:* The attempt to produce a clear wine through racking, fining, or filtering.

# STABILIZATION

*The goal of stabilization and its various techniques—racking, fining, filtering, cold stabilization, and the use of sulfur dioxide—is that once bottled the wine will remain relatively unchanged. Stabilization helps prevent chemical changes that adversely affect a wine's color and clarity as well as microbiological changes that transform it into vinegar or something equally undrinkable.*

*However, stabilization is a relative term. Inexpensive, mass-produced wines are the most thoroughly manipulated in the quest for stability through the use of nearly every possible technique. Fine wines, produced on a smaller scale, are typically less thoroughly manipulated, although sulfur, cold stabilization, fining, and filtering may be used. A clean winery and barrel-aging also help ensure a wine's stability.*

*Racking:* The transfer of wine from one container to another with the purpose of leaving sediment behind.

*Fining:* Adding egg whites or gelatin to remove suspended solids in the wine.

*Filtering:* Pumping the wine through filters to remove solids, residual sugar, dead yeast cells, and bacteria. Filtering has become a controversial practice, as some wine critics and winemakers believe it strips aroma and flavor from the wine.

*Tartrates:* Crystals of potassium acid tartrate that form during fermentation and aging. The crystals attach to the bottom of the cork or fall to the bottom of the bottle. While they look like glass particles, they are harmless and do not affect the taste of the wine in any way. If they are present in a bottle, simply decant the wine off the crystals.

*Cold stabilization:* The process by which a wine is chilled prior to bottling so that the tartrates fall out of the solution and are removed.

*Pomace:* What's left over—skins, stems, seeds, pulp—after the juice or wine is removed. Pomace is distilled into grappa in Italy and marc in France. In the United States, it is usually recycled into the vineyard.

*Lots:* The continuation of the selection process as vineyard blocks, varietals, and different batches of wines are vinified and aged separately as separate lots.

*Bulk wine:* All the lots and barrels that do not make the cut for the final blend and are sold off to other producers.

*Blending:* How the winemaker (oops, winegrower, as the case may be) chooses the best lots and in some cases individual barrels in order to obtain the aromas, flavors, texture, alcohol, and balance desired in the finished wine.

# RESEARCH TOPICS

Look up and read more extensively about:

1. The vinification of wine
2. Viticultural topics such as:
   - climate
   - soil
   - clones
   - canopy management
   - pruning
   - trellising
   - harvest

3. The world's great wine regions and vineyards in:
   - California
   - Bordeaux
   - Burgundy
   - Alsace
   - Loire Valley
   - Germany
   - Italy
   - Spain
   - Australia

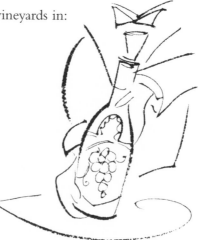

# QUESTIONS

1. In America, if a wine is labeled Chardonnay, by law it must be at
   least _____% Chardonnay.
   a) 50
   b) 75
   c) 95

2. Bordeaux-style blends that do not meet the minimum percent varietal
   requirement are known generally as _____
   wines and are given proprietary names according to the whims of the vintner.

3. Why are some vineyards better than others? _____
   _____
   _____

4. It doesn't matter which grape variety is planted in a specific vineyard. **T or F**

5. What is an AVA? _____
   _____

6. Name several AVAs: _____
   _____

7. Name several sub-AVAs: _____
   _____

8. The more specific a label is in listing region and vineyard, the better the wine is
   apt to be. **T or F**

9. Name some potential dangers to the vine and grapes:

    a)   with two legs:            birds and humans

    b)   with four legs:          _____

    c)   with many legs:         _____

    d)   with no discernible legs:  _____

    e)   with no legs whatsoever:  _____

## Multiple Choice

10. What is *tannin?*

    a)   a method for drying leather

    b)   something you do at the beach

    c)   the "puckery" compound in red wines

11. What is *viticulture?*

    a)   a doctor's throat stick

    b)   a vitamin-obsessed cult

    c)   the science of growing grapes

12. What is *phylloxera?*

    a)   a Greek delicacy

    b)   a toilet-bowl cleaner

    c)   a small plant louse

13. What is a *rootstock?*

    a)   a town in Vermont

    b)   a Wall Street fund in carrot futures

    c)   a native American root onto which a *Vitis vinifera* vine is grafted

14. What are *clones?*

    a)   B-film zombies

    b)   slang for winds that ravage Kansas

    c)   subvarieties of the same grape

15. What is *canopy management?*

    a) a circus job

    b) a weatherman's nightmare

    c) the pruning and trellising of grape vines

16. What is the *crush?*

    a) an orange-flavored drink

    b) the tingly feeling near that certain someone

    c) the harvesting and initial processing of the grapes

17. What is *must?*

    a) a word of command

    b) the smell of an unopened attic

    c) the juice and pulp after crushing

18. What is *free-run juice?*

    a) the latest rap star

    b) O.J. on the run

    c) the result of the first crushing and gentle pressings

19. What is *oak?*

    a) "A-okay" in neo-pig Latin

    b) the sound of a frog with a speech impediment

    c) the wooden barrels used to influence the taste of a wine

20. What is *extended maceration?*

    a) a newest fad in aerobics

    b) state-of-the-art eyelash thickener

    c) leaving the skins in the wine following fermentation

21. What is *residual sugar?*

    a) the resident cutie-pie

    b) plaque's maiden name

    c) sugar remaining in wine after fermentation

22. What is *racking?*

   a) an ancient system of torture

   b) a nasty cough

   c) the transfer of wine from one container to another

23. What is *fining?*

   a) the favorite sport of traffic cops

   b) the process undergone by Miss Doolittle

   c) adding egg whites or gelatin to wine in order
      to clarify it

# ANSWERS

1. b
2. Meritage
3. Great grapes make great wines. Great vineyards make great grapes.
4. False
5. An area recognized by law as an Approved Viticultural Area
6. Alexander Valley, Carneros, Napa Valley, Russian River Valley, etc.
7. Atlas Peak, Howell Mountain, Mount Veeder, Oakville, Rutherford, Spring Mountain, Stag's Leap District, etc.
8. True
9.
    b) wild pigs
    c) insects
    d) fungi, viruses
    e) weather
11–23. c

# MORE QUESTIONS

26. *Tannin* helps red wine _____.

27. *Phylloxera* attacks the _____ of a grape vine.

28. Why plant different *clones?*
    a) aroma
    b) flavor
    c) _____
    d) _____
    e) _____

**29.** Why is canopy management important?_____

_____

_____

_____

_____


**30.** The flavors *oak* imparts to a wine are:

a) butterscotch

b) _____

c) _____

d) _____


**31.** Residual sugar is important in _____ wines.


# MORE ANSWERS

**26.** age

**27.** roots

**28.**

   c) yield

   d) resistance to disease

   e) compatibility with specific rootstocks

**29.** It creates balance in the vine in order to produce the best possible fruit.

**30.**

   b) smokey

   c) toast

   d) vanilla

**31.** dessert

# 4

# White Wine

The odds are overwhelming that 1) white wine is the biggest seller at your local wineshop as well as at your favorite restaurant, and that 2) California Chardonnay is the bestselling white varietal. So much so that California Chardonnay has become synonymous with premium white wine.

## TEN REASONS WHY CALIFORNIA CHARDONNAY IS NUMBER ONE

1. Most California Chardonnay is pretty delicious stuff.
2. Chardonnay is easy to pronounce, California labels are easy to read, and there is a perception of value and quality.
3. Since the wine business is based on giving consumers what they want, we get lots and lots of Chardonnay.
4. White wine, for the most part, is less complex than red wine and more easily appreciated by new wine drinkers.
5. White or "clear" liquids are perceived as "lite" (as in less calories, less of everything), which has been a very significant consumer trend in recent years. White wine has benefited from this trend.

6. Chardonnay is white.

7. Along with this lite trend has been a move toward lighter and healthier foods, which pair better with white wines.

8. White wine is served chilled. Americans love their beverages cold—ice-cold. The only problem with serving wine too cold is that you can't taste it.

9. White wine, for the most part, doesn't benefit from aging. Make it, sell it, and drink it in pretty short order—this is a cycle that benefits the cash flow of everyone in the loop, from the winery to the consumer.

10. White wine tastes good and is fun to drink.

# MEANWHILE, BACK IN HOLLYWOOD

Those starving-artist years back in New York are now sepia-toned and so very romantic as you deposit your check for $24 million for the first film in your three-picture deal. But what to spend it on? Real estate! That's it. A loft in Manhattan's trendy TriBeCa and a ranch in Montana and a winery in Northern California.

# DECISIONS, DECISIONS, DECISIONS

The loft is easy. Hire a hotshot interior designer with great taste and be ready to write checks. The ranch isn't so hard either; everyone you know in Hollywood already has one and a hot tip on a great deal. But the winery is a little tricky, since you want to be more hands-on. That wine thing has you really hooked. Get ready to start making decisions. Lots of decisions:

**Look into your crystal ball. What sells?**
Chardonnay!!! *(Move 4 spaces.)*

**What style of Chardonnay?**
The kind you like to drink: rich, buttery Chardonnay, exquisite in its balanced complexity. *(Move 10 spaces.)*

## But where?

- Napa Valley. It has the brand name, the reputation, and a number of excellent restaurants, but it's crowded and is becoming better known for its reds.
- Sonoma. The land is a little cheaper and you like a number of Chardonnay producers there, but it's a little too rural for your taste.
- Santa Barbara. Great beaches, great vineyards, great Chardonnay producers, but it's too close to L.A.
- Carneros. Shared by the southern extremes of Napa and Sonoma, Carneros is gaining raves for well-structured Chardonnays with complex aromas and flavors of apple, lemon, honey, melon, and spice. Best of all, as you taste a number of Carneros-grown Chardonnays, you like their lively acidity and smooth, silky texture.

Carneros it is! *(Advance Directly to Go and Collect $200.)*

But how are you going to do it?

## Option I

1. Shell out big bucks to buy an undeveloped vineyard site (an old cow pasture) in Carneros. *(Move back 12 spaces.)*
2. Buy a Lexus. *(Lose a turn.)*
3. Hire a vineyard manager. *(Move 2 spaces.)*
4. Plant phylloxera-resistant rootstocks and graft on the Chardonnay clones that will deliver the aromas and flavors you are after. *(Move 9 spaces.)*
5. Sit tight *(do not pass Go for four to six years)* until these vines are sufficiently mature to produce a commercial crop. Listen to your money manager second-guess you.
6. Torture yourself by reading the *Wine Spectator* and seeing the high scores all your competitors are getting. *(Do not pass Go.)*
7. Start interviewing winemakers/winegrowers. *(Move 3 spaces.)*
8. Make another movie. It's a big hit.
9. Start praying to St. Martin of Tours, patron saint of winegrowers, that consumers do not suddenly lose their taste for Chardonnay. *(Lose a turn.)*
10. Take up a hobby while you wait for your vineyard to come on line. *(Lose a turn.)*

# OR

## Option II

1. Sign a long-term contract with a grower, one who owns a proven nearby Chardonnay vineyard, to purchase his grapes. *(Advance directly to Go.)*
2. Hire a winemaker. *(Advance 3 spaces.)*
3. Contract for production and storage space at another winery so that you can make wine. *(Advance 6 spaces.)*
4. Buy new French oak barrels. *(Advance 1 space.)*
5. Make your Chardonnay with the purchased grapes. *(Lose a turn as the wine ages eight to ten months in the barrel and three to four months in the bottle.)*
6. Breathe a sigh of relief when your Chardonnay receives a 95 rating from the *Wine Spectator. (Raise your price and stay out of Jail.)*
7. Host a vintner's dinner at your favorite restaurant in L.A. Invite all your friends and leave a big tip! *(Advance to Go.)*
8. Buy a Land Rover. *(Go directly to Jail.)*
9. Start plans for building your own winery. *(Advance 4 spaces.)*

## The Pros and Cons

### Option I

*Pros:* Total control. If you own the vineyard, you farm it exactly the way you want with no questions asked. It's *your* money, *your* vineyard, *your* grapes, *your* wine.

*Cons:* Your vineyard is a raw site with absolutely no track record of producing Chardonnay. Although it is surrounded by outstanding Chardonnay vineyards, there is no way of knowing if you have bought a great vineyard or a vinegar patch until you start making wine from your own grapes. Do you have the patience to wait four to six years to find out the quality of wine your vineyard is able to produce?

### Option II

*Pros:* Immediate gratification. Purchased grapes from a proven vineyard result in an award-winning wine. The money and praise flow in.

# Hiring a Winemaker

*1. Taste the wines he has made in the past. Do you like them?*

*2. Ask him what wines he likes to drink, collect, or enjoy. Are these wines that you also like to drink, collect, or enjoy?*

*3. Ask him to define quality for you. Does his definition ring true to you?*

*Cons:* Lack of control. For example, the question of yield. The contract you've signed with the grower stipulates a price per ton for his grapes, with a bonus for quality. But tonnage (or yield) is what pays the grower's mortgage on a second home in Hawaii. The grower is motivated to produce a big crop, which may translate into grapes that lack flavor and balance. The greater the number of grape clusters per vine, the harder the vine has to work to ripen the grapes, and the lower the quality of the fruit. You do not want a big yield, you want great fruit. Conflict arrives in the second year of your contract, when Mother Nature delivers a big crop—the vines are loaded with clusters. The grower's eyes light up with dollar signs, as well as visions of a powerboat to go along with that second home. The only solution is to drop fruit—go through the vineyard cutting off 20% of the developing clusters on each vine. The grower cries financial ruin; losing 20% of his crop is a big hit. He offers to drop 5%. You compromise at 12%. The 8% difference in crop size makes a difference in the quality of your wine. Your second vintage receives an 89 rating from the *Wine Spectator*. No one buys your wine; inventory backs up. *(Go directly to Jail.)*

# YOUR DECISION

You decide to play it safe and cover your bets by having it both ways. You sign a long-term contract with the grower that will guarantee you enough grapes to produce 5,000 cases of Chardonnay. At the same time, you start to plant your own vineyard.

# FARMING PRACTICES

You've hired a winegrower, and if wine is indeed made in the vineyard, the decisions about farming practices that have to be made throughout the growing season will hopefully result in great fruit. Just a few of these decisions are: how to deal with pests; which canopy management techniques to employ; whether or not to irrigate or fertilize; and lastly, when to pick. And what about your own vineyard, where you have to make decisions on which rootstocks to plant, which Chardonnay clones to graft, and what spacing to use? Not to mention that you have to start thinking about what to call your winery, how much to charge, what the label is going to look like, who your distributors are going to be, what your marketing plan will entail . . . Whoa!! Let's stay in the vineyard, where the real action is.

# HARVEST WORRIES

Assuming the weather cooperates—which it has a way of doing in California—and there are no major infestations or diseases, you don't really start to worry until the grapes begin to ripen. Then you spend every day in the vineyard, closely following the ripening process and praying for continued good weather, fearful that any of the following disasters might occur at harvest time:

1. If a heat wave hits at harvest, the sugars in the grapes soar and the acidity plummets. The grapes are unbalanced and the wine will be dull and flabby. You may have to acidify.
2. If the weather turns cool, or even cold, the grapes won't ripen. Again, the problem is one of balance. With low sugars, high acids, and immature flavors, the wine will be astringent and green. You are out of luck, since chaptalization is illegal in California. You start praying for a burst of warm weather to ripen the grapes and push the sugars up.

## MAKING A FORTUNE

*A wise man in California once said that the fastest way to make a small fortune in the wine business is to start with a big one.*

*Michael Bonadies*

3. Rain is your greatest fear at harvest time. The result is diluted flavors as the grapes suck up water. And if the rain doesn't stop, rot can set in and ruin the entire crop. Thank God for your second career.

But if you get lucky and the weather holds, then your only worry will be: Is there enough cold beer?

# THE VINIFICATION OF WHITE WINE—MORE DECISIONS

Your luck held. The beer's cold, and the Chardonnay grapes have arrived at the winery in great shape. They are weighed (remember you're paying by the ton) and then dumped into the hopper, which sends whole clusters to the stemmer-crusher. As the stemmer-crusher separates the grapes from their stems and gently breaks the skins, the free-run juice begins to flow. The grapes are transformed into the must, which is kept at a cool temperature, and the winemaking process begins. In not-so-distant times, villagers would dump whole clusters into large vats, jump in naked, and crush the grapes with their feet and bodies. Rumor has it that they had a good time doing this. The human body and foot are perfect crushers; with their padding of muscle, they are able to release the juice without crushing the skins, seeds, and stems, which can release bitter tannins. Mechanical stemmer-crushers are designed to be as gentle as possible.

## Decision #1: Skin Contact?
Skin contact, prior to pressing, is not common for white wines. However, if you have great fruit, you may want several hours of skin contact with the juice in order to heighten the flavors and aromas.
*Your Call:* Since you want a full-flavored Chardonnay, you decide on five hours of skin contact.

## Decision #2: Fermentation Vessel
The fermentation vessels may be either small oak barrels or large temperature-controlled stainless-steel tanks. Today, most white wine fermentation takes place in cooled stainless-steel tanks, since the cooler the fermentation temperature, the greater the preservation of

# THE EVOLUTION OF A WINEGROWER

*"Winegrower" is replacing the title "Winemaker" on many business cards. Is there a contradiction here or simply an evolution in philosophy and practice? Jim Clendenen of Au Bon Climat is one winemaker who subscribes to the shift in belief that recognizes the paramount importance of the vineyard and viticultural practices in determining wine quality.*

*Ten to fifteen years ago, this view would have been heresy in California. "My formula for a successful wine then," says Clendenen, "was ninety percent winemaking skills, five percent the quality of the vineyards and the fruit they produced, and the last five percent custodial cleanliness during vinification." Wine was made in the winery, not in the vineyard. Science and technology were triumphant. Grapes were raw material to be transformed by the winemaker. And wine was made according to the formulas taught at the University of California at Davis, the Harvard of American winemaking, which has educated the majority of American winemakers.*

*But experience is a teacher too. And winemaking is a process of discovery. "Our winemaking skills didn't get better," confesses Clendenen, "the grapes did. And I have to admit that, today, my formula for a successful wine is ninety percent the best possible fruit, five percent winemaking skills, and five percent custodial cleanliness."*

fruit flavor in the finished wine. Oak barrel fermentation also preserves the flavor of the fruit because the small barrels disperse heat.

Barrel fermentation is a complex process during which the wine and wood interact. The barrels not only soften the wine and give it a supple and rich texture, they also add buttery, vanilla, and toast flavors. But if you want a lighter, more delicate Chardonnay, stainless steel is the vessel of choice.

*Your Call:* New French oak barrels cost $600 apiece, and 25 cases of wine per barrel means that to barrel-ferment a production of 5,000 cases of wine, you will have to spend $120,000 to purchase the necessary 200 barrels. But money is no object. You want to make a great Chardonnay with tremendous complexity right out of the gate, and you've got the grapes to do it. Write a check for $120,000 and order new French barrels with a medium char to lend the wine just a hint of spice and smoke.

*Michael Bonadies*

## Decision #3: Yeast—Wild or Cultured?

Fermentation occurs when yeast converts grape sugar to alcohol, carbon dioxide, and heat. Until recently, most California winemakers employed commercial strains of cultured yeast for fermentation. The wild yeast that arrived with the grapes from the vineyard were killed by the addition of sulfur dioxide. Previously thought unreliable, the wild yeast are now being given a chance to show what they can do by more adventuresome winemakers, especially in Chardonnay fermentations.

Wild or cultured, yeast needs three things to make a great wine from great grapes: 1) the right temperature (cool for whites, 50 to 60 degrees); 2) enough sugar to feed on; and 3) an absence of oxygen. Fermentation can take anywhere from a few days to several weeks. A cooler, and thus longer, fermentation typically produces the better wine. Fermentation ends when the yeast has fermented the wine "dry" (converted nearly all the sugar to alcohol).

*Your Call:* You want to err on the side of caution, especially with your first vintage. Wild yeast is a risky choice because of the danger of stuck fermentation (a fermentation that ends before all the sugar is converted to alcohol and is very difficult to restart). Your decision is to use cultured yeast, except for several barrels in which you experiment with wild yeast fermentation to see if wild yeast does add greater complexity to the wine.

## Decision #4: Malolactic Fermentation

You may want to encourage a secondary fermentation: malolactic fermentation. This is a fermentation by lactic bacteria that converts the tart malic acid in wine to the softer lactic acid. This decision depends on the vintage and the relative acidity of the grapes you have harvested, as well as the style of Chardonnay you want to make.

*Your Call:* You enjoy the butteriness and complexity that malolactic fermentation contributes to a wine. You ensure that all of your barrels undergo malolactic fermentation.

## Decision #5: How Much Intervention?

The new Chardonnay is cloudy and unstable. Racking, fining, and filtering may be used individually or in combination to clarify the wine as it begins to age. It may also be cold-stabilized in order to remove tartrates and other solids. But you have some worries about filtering and its reputation for stripping flavor from a wine.

*Your Call:* Philosophically, you favor minimal intervention and an unfiltered wine . . . but economic reality wins out. The risk of the potential problems—such as spoilage, instability, bacterial fermentation, and cloudiness, which can occur in an unfiltered wine—scare you off. After all, this will be your first vintage in the marketplace. You decide to play it safe and lightly filter.

### Decision #6: Aging Vessel

Since you have already decided to barrel-ferment, it makes sense to age the wine in the same barrels. While aging, the wine interacts with the oak, extracting color, flavor, aroma, and tannins. At the same time, evaporation occurs and concentrates the wine, which necessitates a careful watch to top off the barrels and keep them full to prevent oxidation.

*Your Call:* A no-brainer. Your decision to barrel-ferment leads to barrel-aging as well. However, if you had opted for stainless-steel fermentation, then you could have transferred the wine to oak barrels for the aging process.

### Decision #7: Blending

Blending can occur at different times: in the vineyard, as different clones or varieties are harvested together; or in the winery, between different musts or nearly finished wines. If you have barrel-fermented and aged, then every barrel is a little different. The goal of blending is balance, flavor, and aroma. It may take hundreds of trial blends before you find the one that tastes best.

*Your Call:* The blend that tastes best.

Bottling completes the process, with the finished Chardonnay receiving at least several months of bottle aging before being released to the marketplace. Bottle aging allows the wine time to recover from the traumas of fermentation, aging, and bottling, and for the aroma, flavor, and textural components to arrange themselves harmoniously.

# MARKETING—MORE DECISIONS

Now that you've made it, you have to sell it. Five thousand cases (60,000 bottles) doesn't seem like much. So what's the big deal? You've just opened a bottle and it's delicious. Well, the winery isn't named yet, the label's not designed, no distributors have been lined up, and your marketing plan so far consists of "It's delicious." Oh . . .

## Decision #1—Name the Winery

The question is whether or not to play on your celebrity. Yes, but not too obviously. That rules out using your own name, and while you're tempted to use the name of your action-hero character, you know that the studio will want their pound of flesh if you do. So you're back to square one. The no-name winery.

_____

_____Winery

_____Vineyards

_____Cellars

_____Vineyard and Winery

Fill in the blanks. You can't sleep. You've got 5,000 bastard cases of delicious Chardonnay without a last name. Then a brainstorm hits in the middle of the night.

*Your Call:* SIDECAR CELLARS! Inspired by the title of the horror movie that, even though it went straight to video, was your first break: *To Hell in a Sidecar.* Plus, it fits in with your collection of vintage motorcycles and sidecars. Brilliant.

## Decision #2—What's It Going to Cost?

You are about to launch a new product no one has ever heard of, but you've got that celebrity pride thing going on. It can't be too cheap. Plus, *People* magazine has caught wind of your venture and wants an exclusive. A certain amount of free press is a given. But where to price your wine? This is your hardest decision. You want to price it low enough so that it will sell, but not so high that you'll be open to cheap shots from wine critics (you already hate film critics) like "a high-priced celebrity effort not worth the price of admission to a movie."

*Your Call:* Finally you arrive at a pricing that will translate to $24 in a wineshop and approximately $48 on a restaurant winelist.

## Decision #3—Design the Label

Now that you've nailed the name, the label is a breeze.

*Your Call:* You commission a painting of one of your vintage sidecars racing through a vineyard. The celebrity play will be on the back label, where you will sign the mission statement of your winery. But the total packaging, including the label, has to have the look appropriate for a luxury product (which your wine, priced at $24 retail, is).

## Decision #4—Who's Going to Distribute It?

While you are free to sell your wine directly to consumers, wineshops, and restaurants in California, in the rest of the country you are required by law to distribute your wine via what's known as the three-tier system: the winery sells to a state-level distributor, who in turn sells to wineshops and restaurants. That means dealing with a different middleman in every state you want to sell your wine in.

*Your Call:* After consulting with a number of your neighboring vintners and hearing horror stories, you resign yourself to going with a broker in California who will handle

# A RECIPE FOR CHARDONNAY

**Ingredients**

*Ripe Chardonnay grapes*
*Cultured yeast*
*New French oak barrels*
*Medium char*
*Malolactic fermentation*

*It helps to think of a winemaker as a chef.*
  1. *Method of preparation*
     * *The chef may choose to poach, sautée, or grill.*
     * *The winemaker chooses between stainless-steel or barrel fermentation.*
  2. *Seasonings*
     * *The chef may employ salt, pepper, lemon, herbs, wine, butter.*
     * *The winemaker employs:*
       —*oak barrel fermentation and aging to create a more texturally appealing wine.*
       —*new oak barrels to lend oaky aroma and flavor.*
       —*charred barrels to create smokey aroma and flavor.*
       —*cultured yeast and its predictable aroma and flavor contributions.*
       —*malolactic fermentation to soften the wine and increase complexity.*
       —*blending to take advantage of the various aromas, acidity, texture, and levels of alcohol each separate lot will lend to the final blend.*

distribution there, and with small fine-wine-focused distributors in the major markets you have targeted in the rest of the country.

### Decision #5—Marketing Plan

Given your Hollywood star status, the launch of Sidecar Cellars will generate a lot of free publicity in the various medias that cover Hollywood, celebrities, wine, and business. While that's great, you've decided, given the size of your production (small) and your price (fairly high), to build your brand via the winelists of popular high-end restaurants, with the goal of selling 70% of your wine to these restaurants and the remainder (30%) to retail wineshops.

*Your Call:* There's only one option: Hit the streets and put a face behind the bottle. It certainly helps that your face is already known as you visit restaurant after restaurant, pour tastes, and sign autographs for whoever is in charge of buying the wine.

### Decision #6—The Allocation Game

As you sit with a map of the United States and your calculator, you quickly realize that there's no wine for Cleveland, your hometown.

*Your Call:* You try again and come up with:

| Distribution Points | Cases |
| --- | --- |
| WINERY LIBRARY* | 200 |
| CALIFORNIA | 1,500 |
| NEW YORK CITY | 1,000 |
| CHICAGO | 500 |
| HOUSTON/DALLAS | 500 |
| BOSTON (AND NANTUCKET) | 350 |
| MIAMI | 250 |
| ASPEN/VAIL | 250 |
| CLEVELAND | 250 |
| FRIENDS AND COLLEAGUES | 200 |

*The 200 cases reserved for your winery library are intended for your own drinking pleasure, entertaining visiting wine buyers, donations to charity auctions, winemaker dinners, and emergencies like White House State Dinners or when your favorite restaurateur begs for more wine after selling through his allocation.

The anticipation and excitement are building. Your fans want your wine, but only 1,500 cases have been slated for a select number of retail wineshops around the country. They'll just have to find a restaurant that has placed your wine on its list. This is a great problem to have until *Wine & Spirits,* Robert Parker, Jr., and the *Wine Spectator* all give your first release a score of 95 or higher. All hell breaks loose as *everyone*—from the White House down to your high school drama teacher—wants a case of your wine. You disconnect your phone, reach for a beer, and wonder how you can buy more Chardonnay grapes next year.

# HOW TO TASTE AND APPRECIATE
# WHITE WINE (OR ANY OTHER)

It's time to move from tasting to appreciation. Of course, you have to taste in order to appreciate. But now is the time to start putting it all together—the aromas, bouquets, flavors, textures, and personalities of the wines you taste in order to develop a sense and taste memory. This memory results only from the experience of tasting as many wines as you can. Concentration is required each and every time you taste in order for your sensory experiences of these wines and your descriptions of them to become stored in the recesses of your brain.

It is a good habit to take notes when you taste wine. A notebook helps keep all your notes in one place. It's fun to see how much better a taster you've become by the time you reach the last page. Unless you have very, very tiny handwriting, allow one wine per page. Before you know it, you'll be filling up the page.

Why bother to write down all your impressions? If you enjoy tasting and begin to get good at it, you are going to be curious about how a Carneros Chardonnay differs from a Russian River Chardonnay, and how a French Chardonnay differs from an Australian Chardonnay, and how a 1996 Chardonnay differs from a 1997. Don't forget to include the date of your tasting. If you have the opportunity to taste the same wine one year later, it will be very interesting to compare your notes to see not only how the wine has changed but also how practice has made you a better taster with a greater appreciation for wine.

Language is the medium we use to express our sensory impressions. The Wine Aroma Wheel (see page 25), with its ready-made vocabulary, is a great starting point. But it is only a starting point and one to which you shouldn't feel restricted.

As you taste, think of wine in tactile terms too. Wine has textural qualities that you experience on your tongue and in your mouth. These can be described, for example, as light or heavy, lean or fat, full or thin, silky or harsh, linear or flabby, crisp or mellow, round or angular, just to mention a few. I'm sure you can think of others.

Personality comes into play with wine as well. It is perfectly appropriate to describe a wine as seductive or serious, sensuous or austere, engaging or reticent, in-your-face or shy, mysterious or boring, exotic or plain.

The key is to concentrate and to believe in your own sensory perceptions and language skills. It's *your* experience, not that of the person sitting next to you or the wine critic whose column you have just read. Start to believe in your own tasting abilities and have some fun.

# MAJOR WHITE WINE GRAPE VARIETIES

### Chardonnay
**In the Vineyard:** Easy to grow in almost any type of soil, it ripens early, bears a consistent crop, and is resistant to cold. Frost can be a problem due to early bud break.

**History:** Its "homeland" is Burgundy, where Charlemagne ordered it planted so that he could drink a wine that wouldn't stain his beard. It is believed to have originated in Syria and Lebanon. Today, it is the single most popular variety and is grown all over the world.

**As a Wine:** Winemakers love it. Chardonnay is the most malleable of grapes and responds well to a wide range of winemaking techniques. Its marriage with oak results in the richest and most complex Chardonnays.

**Aromas and Flavors:** Apple, butterscotch, buttery, lemon-lime, melon, nutty, pear, smokey, spice, steely, tropical fruit, and vanilla.

**Styles:** Typically a rich and complex dry wine. Major stylistic differences are due to stainless-steel fermentation/aging versus barrel fermentation/aging.

**Food Pairing:** Goes with nearly everything. Less oaky Chardonnays are most suitable with lighter fish and shellfish dishes, such as poached or sautéed preparations. The very oaky and buttery Chardonnays go better with grilled foods, particularly swordfish, salmon, halibut, tuna, chicken, veal, and pork.

**Top Producers:** Au Bon Climat, Beringer, Byron, Chalk Hill, Chateau Montelena, Far Niente, Jordan, Joseph Phelps, Kistler, Marcassin, Matanzas Creek, Meridian, Morgan, Patz & Hall, Peter Michael, Qupé, Sanford, Sonoma-Cutrer, Talbott, ZD.

**Personality:** Elected most popular.


### Sauvignon Blanc (Fumé Blanc)
**In the Vineyard:** Grows well in warmer climates but produces steely and racy wines in cooler ones. Highly susceptible to *Botrytis cinerea* and oidium (powdery mildew). It is often grown in conjunction with Sémillon, with which it is frequently blended.

**History:** The white of Bordeaux, but excels as well in the Loire Valley (Sancerre, Pouilly-Fumé) of France, where it produces crisp, steely wines. Robert Mondavi turned Sauvignon Blanc around in California when he gave it some oak aging and a new name: Fumé Blanc.

**As a Wine:** Dry, crisp, and refreshing. A wine to be drunk young.

***Aromas and Flavors:*** Apricot, bell pepper, citrus, floral, grass, hay, melon, mineral, peach, smokey, and straw.

***Styles:*** Can produce excellent sweet wines but is most commonly fermented dry. To oak or not to oak has a tremendous impact on the finished wine, as does the decision to make a 100% Sauvignon Blanc or to blend it with Sémillon and/or Chardonnay. The trend in California today is toward wines with greater fruit and floral aromas and flavors.

***Food Pairing:*** Perfect for Southwestern dishes. Sauvignon Blanc stands up to, and pairs well with, chilis, salsas, and corn-based dishes. It is also a good bet with Asian preparations and dishes served with a vinaigrette.

***Top Producers:*** Babcock, Cain, Cakebread, Chalk Hill, Dry Creek, Duckhorn, Frog's Leap, Kunde, Markham, Matanzas Creek, Murphy-Goode, Rochioli, Spottswoode.

***Personality:*** Ready to party! Good, easy sipping.

## Riesling

Also known as White Riesling and Johannisberg Riesling.

***In the Vineyard:*** A late budder and ripener, it is able to survive extreme cold and thrive at the northern limits of where vines can grow and still ripen grapes. Its greatest strength lies in its ability to ripen to very high sugar levels without losing its racy acidity and balance.

***History:*** Of Germanic origin and mentioned by Roman writers as early as the first century A.D. It is the grape of Germany's Rhine and Mosel valleys and the one noble variety that has lent itself to successful crossings with other varieties, producing such hybrids as Müller-Thurgau and Scheurebe. Riesling is also an important grape in Alsace, California, and upstate New York. It is susceptible to *Botrytis cinerea* (noble rot—more on this in the chapter on dessert wines), which concentrates its flavors and results in some of the greatest sweet wines in the world.

***As a Wine:*** Vibrant and racy thanks to its lively acidity, which also enables it to be a long-lived white. Never sees new oak and excels as a sweet wine. A great wine that hasn't caught on with Americans due to the confusing nomenclature of German wine labels and the sweet/dry thing.

***Aromas and Flavors:*** Apricot, floral, honey, minerals, peach, petrol, and spice.

***Styles:*** Sweet or dry. In Germany and California, the sweet versions are where it's at. Riesling is fermented dry in Alsace.

**Food Pairing:** A dry and crisp Riesling is ideal with trout, sole, turbot, crab, lobster, and halibut. A rich or full-style Riesling is best with veal or chicken or a mushroom sauce. Dessert-style Rieslings are great with fruit desserts.

**Top Producers:** Bonny Doon, Handley, Joseph Phelps, Navarro, Stony Hill, Trefethen.

**Personality:** A nervous, high-strung genius type. Hard to get to know, but once you do—wow!

## Chenin Blanc

**In the Vineyard:** A vigorous producer easily adapted to many soil types. A late ripener susceptible to rot.

**History:** Grown in the Loire Valley since the ninth century.

**As a Wine:** You name it, Chenin Blanc can do it: incredibly intense, long-lived sweet wines; dry wines with exotic aromas; sparkling wines, and jug wines. Typically high in acid.

**Aromas and Flavors:** Chalk, floral, guava, honey, lemon, melon, peach, pear, slate, and vanilla.

**Styles:** Many.

**Food Pairing:** Its wonderful balance of richness and acidity makes Chenin Blanc perfect for rich foods that are in need of a little acidity to lighten them up, such as fried fish or chicken, salmon with a beurre blanc, or duck confit.

**Top Producers:** Chappellet, Girard.

**Personality:** Multiple personalities but a personal favorite—if you get a chance, check out a Savennières from the Loire Valley. Yum.

## Viognier

**In the Vineyard:** Capricious and difficult to grow, with small, unreliable yields. It is a miracle this variety has survived.

**History:** Until recently, Viognier was in danger of extinction. Barely 80 acres were left in cultivation in the northern Rhône Valley of France, where it produces Condrieu and is blended into Côte Rôtie, a red. Then it was discovered by Californians, and it has since experienced a rebirth as the up-and-coming new white variety.

**As a Wine:** When it decides to produce a crop of grapes, it can deliver a wine many have called "the greatest white wine you've never heard of."

**Aromas and Flavors:** Apricot, honeysuckle and other blossoms, minerals, peach, and pear.

**Styles:** Full-bodied and seductive, rich and exotic.

**Food Pairing:** Ideal as an aperitif, with full-flavored fish or shellfish dishes such as bouillabaisse, or those with lobster, crab, or crayfish sauces.

**Top Producers:** Alban, Arrowood, Calera, Joseph Phelps, Qupé.

**Personality:** Mysterious and enchanting. Be the first one on your block to taste it.

### Gewürztraminer

**In the Vineyard:** Pink or nearly red grapes. An early ripener but with erratic yields. Prone to virus and frost damage.

**History:** Believed to have originated in the Italian Tyrol, it thrives in Alsace and has become an important variety in the cooler regions of California.

**As a Wine:** Easily one of the most intense and distinctive wines when well made. Typically fermented dry, but in certain vintages it produces excellent sweet wines.

**Aromas and Flavors:** *Gewürz* means "spice," and that is one of its important descriptors, in addition to apple, citrus, clove, floral, honeysuckle, lychee, mineral, pear, and smokey.

**Styles:** Dry or off-dry.

**Food Pairing:** Excels with rich preparations such as foie gras, pâtés, terrines, sweetbreads, and cream sauces. It is also very good as an aperitif.

**Top Producers:** Fetzer (their dry version), Martinelli, Navarro.

**Personality:** Exotic.

### Sémillon

**In the Vineyard:** While grown all over the world, it grows *well* in only a handful of places: Bordeaux, Northern California, Washington State, and Australia's Hunter Valley. Elsewhere it produces flabby, insipid wines. Its thin skin is a favorite of *Botrytis cinerea*.

**History:** The major white wine grape, along with Sauvignon Blanc, of Bordeaux.

**As a Wine:** When blended with Sauvignon Blanc, it adds complexity and smoothes out Sauvignon Blanc's occasional rough edges. On its own, it is best as a dessert wine that can develop tremendous complexity with age.

**Aromas and Flavors:** Citrus, honey, melon, orange, pear, and spice.

**Styles:** Most famous as a dessert-style wine. In dry versions in California, it produces excellent wines when barrel-fermented.

**Food Pairing:** In its sweet version, the classic match is with foie gras or Roquefort cheese.

**Top Producers:** Joseph Phelps (a dessert wine version), Kalin, Signorello.
**Personality:** A late bloomer. Plays second fiddle to Sauvignon Blanc in blends. When given the opportunity to shine as a dessert wine, it has few peers.

### Anything but Chardonnay

Chardonnay's popularity was bound to provoke a backlash. When you're elected "most popular," everyone disses you behind your back. Poor Chardonnay. The anti-Chardonnay movement fostered by certain Chardonnay-challenged winemakers and sommeliers is known as ABC, or Anything But Chardonnay. Sure, Chardonnay rules, but it tastes great too. The ABC zealots do have a point, though: there are white wines other than Chardonnay. For example, Chenin Blanc, Gewürztraminer, Marsanne, Pinot Blanc, Pinot Gris, Riesling, Roussanne, Sauvignon Blanc, Sémillon, and Viognier. When was the last time you tried one of these non-Chardonnays? And how many of them have never passed your lips? As consistently good as Chardonnay is, there are clearly other whites that deliver wonderful drinking pleasure as well.

# DO WHITE WINES AGE?

Yes and no. The vast majority of whites are meant to be drunk young. White Burgundies and better California Chardonnays will drink well for ten years and beyond. The great sweet whites made from Chenin Blanc, Riesling, and Sémillon can live for decades. Acidity and/or residual sugar are the keys to a white wine's ability to age gracefully. As a rule, most white wines are meant to be drunk within a year or two of bottling.

# CONCLUSION—IS IT DRY?

How many times have you wondered or asked that question when confronted with an unknown wine. Even an unknown Chardonnay. Relax. The overwhelming majority of wines produced are vinified dry.

But it certainly isn't dry in California. It is wintertime and El Niño is dumping tons of water on the vineyards. You're alarmed, but your vineyard manager calms you. She explains that the vines are dormant, the rain won't damage them, and her crew is just waiting for a break in the weather to prune.

Your film career should be so fortunate. Your last two films have been bombs, and while people return your calls, no one wants to have lunch or meet with you. And since your name no longer guarantees instant reservations at New York's hottest restaurants, you put your TriBeCa loft on the market.

# RESEARCH TOPICS

## Other Important White Wine Varietals

As a research project, look up and read about the following:

- Marsanne
- Roussanne
- Scheurebe
- Pinot Gris (also known in Italy as Pinot Grigio)
- Pinot Blanc
- Muscat
- Trebbiano
- Melon de Bourgogne

## Important White Wine Regions

As a research project, look up and read about the following:

- Burgundy and its great white wine vineyards
- Alsace
- Germany
- Loire Valley
- Australia
- New Zealand
- New York State
- Oregon

- Washington State
- Sonoma County
- Napa Valley
- California's Central Coast

# SUGGESTED TASTINGS

If you have a good local wineshop, ask them to recommend the various styles of wine for your tastings.

## Chardonnay

- oak versus stainless steel
- lightly oaked versus heavily oaked
- barrel-fermented versus non-barrel-fermented, both aged in oak
- French versus California versus Australia
- Napa versus Sonoma versus Central Coast
- single vineyard versus a blend of vineyards
- 100% malolactic versus partial malolactic
- comparing different vintages of the same wine

## Chardonnay Versus Anything But Chardonnay

With Chardonnay as the standard, taste it against other varieties in order to experience their similarity to, or difference from, Chardonnay:

- Sauvignon Blanc
- Viognier
- Riesling
- Sémillon
- Chenin Blanc
- Gewürztraminer
- Pinot Gris
- White Blends

## Sauvignon Blanc

- oak versus stainless steel
- 100% Sauvignon Blanc versus a blend of Sauvignon Blanc and Sémillon
- Loire Valley versus Bordeaux versus California versus New Zealand

## Riesling

- Germany versus Alsace versus California
- dry versus sweet
- Riesling versus a hybird such as Scheurebe or Müller-Thurgau

## Chenin Blanc

- Loire Valley versus California
- dry versus sweet

## Viognier

- Condrieu versus California

## Gewürztraminer

- Alsace versus California
- dry versus sweet

## Sémillon

- Bordeaux versus California versus Australia
- 100% Sémillon versus a blend with Sauvignon Blanc
- dry versus sweet

# QUESTIONS

1. Name several reasons for the popularity of Chardonnay in the United States:
   a) <u>tastes great</u>
   b) _____
   c) _____
   d) _____
   e) _____

2. Today, the crushing of grapes is done by:
   a) naked villagers
   b) the tender feet of virgins
   c) retired professional wrestlers
   d) mechanical stemmer-crushers

3. For what reason, in the making of white wine, might you want a couple of hours of skin contact with the juice?

   _____

   _____

   _____

   _____

4. Which of the following are used as fermentation vessels?
   a) oak barrel
   b) empty beer keg
   c) charred pine cask
   d) stainless-steel tank

5. Which of the following qualities are given to white wine by small oak barrel fermentation and aging?
   a) buttery and rich
   b) light and delicate
   c) tannic and chewy

d) vanilla and toast

e) young and green

6. The growing acceptance of the title "Winegrower" is
a result of:

a) boredom with the title "Winemaker"

b) a ploy by printers to sell more business cards

c) recognition of the fact that great wine starts in the vineyard

7. Which phrase best describes the philosophy of a winegrower?

a) farm for big yields

b) farm for flavor and balance

c) farm for hard tannins

d) farm for fame and fortune

8. As a result of undergoing malolactic fermentation, wine tastes:

a) harder

b) more sour

c) softer and richer

d) sweeter

9. What are some adjectives you might use to describe a wine?

| | | |
|---|---|---|
| a) crisp | j) boring | s) full |
| b) velvety | k) shy | t) light |
| c) fat | l) nutty | u) spicy |
| d) angular | m) earthy | v) delicious |
| e) mellow | n) yummy | w) wild |
| f) in-your-face | o) crass | x) simple |
| g) seductive | p) fruity | y) all of the above |
| h) plain | q) gorgeous | z) exactly half of |
| i) austere | r) engaging | the above |

**10.** List some characteristics of *Chardonnay* in terms of:
Aromas and Flavors: _____
Styles: _____

**11.** List some characteristics of *Sauvignon Blanc* in terms of:
Aromas and Flavors: _____
Styles: _____

**12.** List some characteristics of *Riesling* in terms of:
Aromas and Flavors: _____
Styles: _____

**13.** List some characteristics of *Chenin Blanc* in terms of:
Aromas and Flavors: _____
Styles: _____

**14.** List some characteristics of *Viognier* in terms of:
Aromas and Flavors: _____
Styles: _____

**15.** List some characteristics of *Gewürztraminer* in terms of:
Aromas and Flavors: _____
Styles: _____

**16.** List some characteristics of *Sémillon* in terms of:
Aromas and Flavors _____
Styles: _____

**17.** True or false: Most white wines are meant to be drunk young. **T or F**

# ANSWERS

1. b) easy to pronounce

   c) more easily appreciated than red wine

   d) perceived as "lite" or healthier

   e) served chilled

2. d

3. To heighten flavors and aromas

4. a and d

5. a and d

6. c

7. b

8. c

9. All of these and more!!!

10–16. Refer to text, pages 78 through 82.

17. True

# | 5 |

# RED WINE

I am a red wine drinker. Especially California reds: Cabernet Sauvignon, Pinot Noir, Syrah, Merlot, Zinfandel, and every other red grown and vinified in California. And I happily confess that other reds, such as sensual Burgundies, classic Bordeaux, Rhône beauties, and Italian charmers—not to mention delicious reds from South Africa, Spain, Portugal, Greece, Lebanon, Argentina, Chile, Australia, Oregon, Washington State, and Long Island—have passed my lips. I love red wine. This is a fun chapter for me, and I hope it will be for you as well.

## TEN REASONS PLUS ONE WHY *I THINK* RED WINE IS MORE FUN THAN WHITE

1. I love the way red wine looks, smells, and tastes.
2. Red wines have more complex aromas and flavors.
3. Red wines offer a greater variety of flavors and styles.
4. Red wine grapes lend themselves to blending, which results in even more interesting types of red wines.
5. Inexpensive red wines are, as a rule, across the board better values than inexpensive whites.
6. Red wine ages. You always have something to talk about at boring dinner parties if the host serves a red with any bottle age.
7. Red wine is for the impatient. You don't have to wait for it to chill.

8. Red meat.
9. Health claims that red wine is good for your heart, thus enabling one to justify increased consumption of red meat.
10. Everyone else loves white.
11. California Cabernet Sauvignon, Pinot Noir, Syrah, Merlot, and Zinfandel.

# MEANWHILE, BACK IN MONTANA

You sit on your porch overlooking thousands of acres of scenery and too many steers to count, sipping a Chardonnay—Sidecar Cellars Soft Tail Vineyard Chardonnay—made from the grapes grown in your own vineyard and vinified in your brand-new winery. Finally! And as you taste it beside the Chardonnay you made from purchased grapes, which is damn good, you like the wine your vineyard has delivered a hell of a lot more. So do the wine critics. *(Stay out of Jail and raise your prices.)*

But later that evening, as you toss huge steaks onto the grill and your guests enjoy the Chardonnay, you grow increasingly bummed that you don't have a Sidecar Cellars red to serve with dinner.

So you want to make a red wine. Which one? Cabernet Sauvignon, the wine you love to drink with charcoal-grilled steak. *(Move 6 spaces.)*

**What have you learned from your Chardonnay experience?**
- You were terribly impatient waiting for your new vineyard to come on-line.
- The ups and downs of buying grapes were frustrating. You didn't like not having total control over the farming practices.
- You have built brand loyalty and demand by making high-quality wines and by focusing on placing your Chardonnays on restaurant winelists.
- Your film career is in the toilet. Absolutely no one will return your calls. But every wine lover in Hollywood is calling your agent trying to score more of your Chardonnay.
- Your winemaker is the star of this show.

**What are your red wine opportunities?**
- A number of grape contracts from top Cabernet Sauvignon vineyards and growers in Napa Valley are up for sale. No need to be patient here, but someone else is in control.

- A relatively small Cabernet Sauvignon specialist, because of a bad back and advancing years, has put his label and its renowned Napa Valley hillside vineyard up for sale. You're talking big bucks here.
- There is a vineyard site on your property in Carneros that might be perfect for Pinot Noir. And your winegrower is hot to trot for Pinot Noir. You know all about how important it is to keep a star happy. *(Move 12 spaces.)*

**So which one will it be? Roll those dice!**

**Option I**
1. Buy up the available contracts.
2. Plan to make and market a Napa Valley Cabernet Sauvignon that blends the grapes from several of the valley's best Cabernet Sauvignon vineyards.
3. Get bids on open-top fermenters, the construction of an additional barrel room, and everything else you need to make red wine.
4. Taste a Cabernet Sauvignon your winegrower made at his last job. No one's perfect. Hire an assistant winemaker who has worked extensively with Cabernet Sauvignon.
5. Sell the Lexus and buy a Mercedes coupe.

# OR

**Option II**
1. Taste the wines the Cabernet Sauvignon specialist has produced over the last several vintages as well as some older ones. Do you still love them?
2. If yes, check the auction catalogues to see what prices his older vintages are bringing.
3. Talk to your banker about a *big* loan. Your last two films bombed, and your days of $24 million per picture are over. As a matter of fact, right now you'd work for scale.
4. Get bids on open-top fermenters, the construction of an additional barrel room, and everything else you need to make red wine.
5. Taste a Cabernet Sauvignon your winegrower made at his last job. No one's

perfect. Hire an assistant winemaker who has worked extensively with Cabernet Sauvignon.

6. Give your vineyard manager a raise. She's done an incredible job with your Chardonnay vineyard.

7. Start tasting other Napa Cabernet Sauvignons to check out the competition. And even check out a few Bordeaux.

8. Sell the Lexus and buy a used pickup.

# OR

## Option III

1. Taste a Pinot Noir your winemaker has made in his spare time. Give him a raise.

2. Talk to your banker about a small loan.

3. Plant phylloxera-resistant rootstocks and graft on the Pinot Noir clones that will deliver the aromas, flavors, and structure your winegrower wants in the final blend.

4. Give your vineyard manager a raise. She's done an incredible job with your Chardonnay vineyard.

5. Sit tight *(do not pass Go for four to six years)* until these vines produce a commercial crop. Start drinking Pinot Noir and expand your horizons while checking out the potential competition.

6. Sell the Lexus and buy a brand-new Harley Fat Boy.

## The Pros and Cons

## Option I

*Pros*

1. Immediate gratification. Purchased grapes from proven vineyards and growers allow you to make a terrific wine right out of the box.

2. You make a splash with quality and quantity, as you're able to contract for enough grapes to produce 15,000 cases—plenty to keep your loyal customers happy and win new ones.

3. With the vineyards in question representing prime sub-AVAs in Napa Valley—Stag's Leap District, Rutherford, and Oakville—you're able to make and market a wine that showcases the best of Napa Valley Cabernet Sauvignon.

4. The money flows in.

## Cons

1. Lack of control. Again you're faced with the question of how to manage the issues of farming practices, yield, and quality when you don't own the vineyards. Remember that the grower is paid for his grapes by the ton. Even though you've done your research and discovered that none of the growers owns a second home in Hawaii (only a time-share up at Lake Tahoe), the lack of control troubles you.

2. Your agent has stopped calling except to request more Chardonnay.


## Option II

### Pros

1. A proven vineyard with a great reputation and a legion of fans and collectors. You're buying what amounts to a brand name.

2. You love the name of this beautiful vineyard—Ranch Vineyard—plus you've been a fan of its wines ever since you first discovered the joys of reds.

3. The vineyard is planted primarily to Cabernet Sauvignon, with blocks of Merlot and Cabernet Franc. The average age of the vines is twenty-two years.

4. Production averages 10,000 cases per year. There will be enough to keep your loyal restaurant accounts happy and to take a shot at the retail market, where the vineyard has enjoyed a solid reputation for years.

5. Recent vintages still aging in the barrel enable you to hit the market immediately with Sidecar Cellars Ranch Vineyard Cabernet Sauvignon.

6. Total control. If you own the vineyard, you farm it exactly the way you want with no questions asked. It's *your* money, *your* vineyard, *your* grapes, *your* wine.

7. You love the wines this vineyard has produced over the years.

8. Selling the small winery facility and adjacent Zinfandel vineyard will allow you to immediately recoup a portion of the purchase price.

## Cons

1. You're paying for a proven vineyard with a great reputation, a legion of fans and collectors, and what amounts to a brand name. We're talking big, big bucks for a hillside covered with grape vines.

2. The wine critics will be out to get you. You can see the headlines now: HOLLYWOOD TAKES OVER, RAPES AND PILLAGES MOM AND POP WINERY. After the treatment of your last two movies by the critics, you're convinced there is a conspiracy afloat.

3. Potential backlash from the fans: "Hollywood sucks."

4. With a production of 10,000 cases there are two potential problems: a) if the wine you make isn't a hit and demand won't support the price you need to get in order to service your loan, it will be time to raid your savings; and b) if the wine you make is a huge hit, you're back in the allocation game of trying to make everyone happy without enough wine ever to succeed.

5. Your agent has stopped calling. Requests for more Chardonnay now arrive via e-mail.


## Option III

### Pros

1. Total control. You can sit on your porch and watch the vineyard farmed exactly the way you want.

2. It will definitely improve your view from the porch.

3. You're beginning to appreciate Pinot Noir.

4. The challenge appeals to you.

5. While it won't be cheap, it won't take millions.

6. You will keep your winemaker happy.

### Cons

1. Your vineyard is a raw site with absolutely no track record for producing Pinot Noir. Although it is contiguous to two outstanding Pinot Noir vineyards and shares with them a similar soil profile and exposure, there is still no way of knowing if you have planted a great vineyard or a vinegar patch until you start making wine from your own grapes.

2. You'll have to wait four to six years to find out the quality of wine

your vineyard is able to produce, but these days you have plenty of time on your hands.

3. Pinot Noir's fickle nature may drive you crazy. It is probably the most difficult grape to grow and vinify successfully.

4. Talk about allocation headaches. Even when the vineyard comes on line full-bore, its maximum production will be 1,500 cases.

5. Your agent calls! He's heard you've sold your loft in New York and wants to know if your Knick season tickets are for sale as well. He has a hot new client who loves basketball and . . . You not so calmly instruct your agent where to stick the tickets, his phone, and the last case of Chardonnay you sent him.

# YOUR DECISIONS

It's springtime in wine country. The wild mustard is in bloom, bud break has occurred, and the vines have begun growing new vegetation. The only worry other than your film career—ex-career—is an early frost that would kill the new growth. On a rosier front, beef prices are up and demand for your Chardonnay has never been stronger. While you're not yet ready to give up on the silver screen, it's clearly time to throw yourself into something new—like red wine—in a big way.

**Decision #1: Grape Source**

Your choices: 1) go the contract route again, a lower-cost entry into the world of red wine, 2) spend big bucks for the brand-name Cabernet Sauvignon vineyard and total control, or 3) sit tight and wait for the Pinot Noir vineyard to produce.

*Your Call:* You decide to: 1) buy the Cabernet Sauvignon vineyard and reach out to its fans and collectors by throwing a party to celebrate your purchase, and 2) plant the Pinot Noir vineyard to keep your winemaker happy.

**Decision #2: The Grapes**

Will your new Ranch Vineyard Cabernet Sauvignon be:

1. 100% Cabernet Sauvignon?

*or*

2. Cabernet Sauvignon blended with Merlot and Cabernet Franc?

*Michael Bonadies*

3. A Meritage wine in which no single varietal needs to be 75% of more of the final blend?

*Your Call:* You rule out Meritage immediately, since historically the vineyard has produced Cabernet Sauvignon wines and that's the varietal name you want on the label. But what about the marketing angle provided by a 100% Cabernet Sauvignon? There's some appeal here, but after tasting several 100% Cabernets versus the wines the vineyard has produced in the past, you find the blended wines much more pleasurable. Stick with tradition. Number 2 it is.

## Decision #3: Style of Wine

What style of wine do you want to make? A big, brawny, tannic, age-worthy red? Or a more accessible red, one with elegant fruit, layers of complex flavors, approachable tannins, yet the ability to age gracefully.

*Your Call:* You started off liking big, obvious reds, but now you find yourself preferring more elegant ones. So:

1. The first Ranch Vineyard Cabernets from the early 1980s were big, tannic monsters, and while they have become more accessible in style over the years, you want (and sense the market also wants) an even richer, more accessible, and more elegant wine. Elegance and accessibility win out.

2. The Pinot Noir you're not sure about. You are several years away from making one and are still tasting your way through the major California Pinot Noir producers. There is such a range of styles, aromas, and flavors . . . and you are seduced by all of them.

# FARMING PRACTICES

Over the winter you huddle with your vineyard manager and winemaker, agonizing over the dilemma phylloxera presents at the Ranch Vineyard. The newer vineyard blocks, planted on the susceptible AxR #1 rootstock, are showing symptoms of a phylloxera infestation. Luckily, the bulk of the vineyard is planted on the more resistant St. George rootstock. Do you try to get another year or two out of the infected vines?

You decide to rip out the infected vines after this fall's harvest and replant the blocks with new rootstock, taking the opportunity to increase the vineyard's percentage of Merlot.

As the winter rains end and spring arrives, you're worrying about your Chardonnay, Cabernet Sauvignon, and Pinot Noir vineyards plus the weather, phylloxera, and whether or not you should face up to the dawning reality that your screen career is over, done with, kaput. But your luck holds, at least in terms of grapes. It is a perfect summer, which fuels speculation that this might be the vintage of the century. Fall approaches, and you harvest the Merlot and Cabernet Franc and begin to vinify them. But you have to wait for the Cabernet Sauvignon, a notoriously late ripener, as the weather turns cool and the grapes stop ripening. Cabernet Sauvignon, like other reds, is harvested at higher sugar levels and lower acid levels than whites. So you wait and wait. Every day you listen to the weather, praying for a warming trend and hoping the rains hold off. Rain is the last thing you want because it can dilute the grapes as well as induce rot. Finally, your prayers are answered. The weather warms, grape sugars rise, and you begin to harvest.

# CRUSH!

Your winery, now just a couple of years old, is rocking. The radio is blasting, the beer is cold, new French barrels with this year's fermenting Chardonnay are stacked to the ceiling, open-topped fermenters are bubbling with fermenting Merlot and Cabernet Franc, and the Cabernet Sauvignon grapes from the Ranch Vineyard are arriving by the trailer-load. Your winegrower is looking stressed.

# THE VINIFICATION OF RED WINE

The same general principles outlined for white wine in the previous chapter also work for red wine vinification. The yeast attacks the sugars in the grape juice and converts them into alcohol, carbon dioxide, and heat. But there are some important differences in making red wine.

## The Major Differences Between Making Red and White

*Fermentation Vessel:* While white wines are fermented in closed vessels—stainless-steel tanks or barrels—red wines are usually fermented in large open-topped stainless-steel fermenters.

**Maceration:** The foremost goal in making red wine is the extraction of color, aroma, flavor, and tannin from the grape skins. This is accomplished through:

*Skin Contact:* Skin contact for reds extends well beyond the few hours a white wine might see prior to fermentation. With red wines, skin contact with the juice extends through and perhaps beyond fermentation.

*Maceration:* Red wines are fermented at higher temperatures (mid-80s for Cabernet versus mid-50s for Chardonnay). High temperatures and alcohol produced during fermentation are the agents that aid the extraction of color, aroma, flavor, and tannin from the grape skins. The longer the extraction or maceration, the greater the amount of flavor, color, and tannin in the wine.

*Extended Maceration:* This occurs when the newly fermented wine is left in contact with the skins following fermentation, usually for a period of about two weeks. Extended maceration initially produces lots of short, bitter tannins. Over the two-week period, they link up with other tannins and color molecules, producing softer tannins and a more accessible, less astringent wine with deeper color and richer, more complex aromas and flavors.

**Oxygen:** While oxygen is the enemy of white wines during fermentation and aging, it is one of the key influences in a red wine's ability to age gracefully. Red wines are carefully exposed to air throughout fermentation and aging in order to rid them of off-odors and encourage the development of their aroma and bouquet.

**Barrel Aging:** As a rule, red wines are barrel-aged far more frequently and for a longer period than whites. Important decisions have to be made concerning the proportions of new oak, French or American barrels, and the degree of char. All these decisions are made by the winemaker in order to bring about the desired aromas, flavors, and textures. Wood tannins and vanilla-like compounds are extracted from the wood during the aging process, with greater amounts being extracted from new barrels than from old ones.

**Malolactic Fermentation:** Malolactic fermentation is far more common in red wines than in whites. It plays a very important part in allowing red wines to develop their full complexity.

**Bottle Aging:** Red wines typically undergo a longer period of bottle aging at the winery before being released than do whites.

# VINIFICATION DECISIONS

### Decision #1: Managing Extraction

The rate and degree of extraction are important variables in determining the style and final quality of a red wine. The biggest challenge results from the cap—the mass of skin, pulp, and seeds that rises to the top of the juice once fermentation begins and carbon diox-

## PASSIONATE ABOUT PINOT

*Everyone wants more. More California Pinot Noir. That's right, and no, it's not a typo. We're waving the flag proud and high, impressed and totally seduced by how good our homegrown Pinot from California has become.*

*Paul Masson was the first to grow and vinify Pinot Noir in Santa Cruz in the late 1800s from vine cuttings he had brought over in a suitcase from Burgundy. But the first Pinot Noir that brought acclaim was André Tchelistcheff's legendary 1946 Beaulieu Vineyards Pinot Noir, produced from fruit grown in the Carneros region. However, in spite of subsequent and often successful Pinot efforts by Martin Ray in Santa Cruz, Hanzell and Joseph Swan in Sonoma in the 1950s and '60s, by the early '70s Pinot Noir in California was a variety facing economic extinction. Its price per ton had fallen by 75%, and its reputation was so poor that wineries bottled and sold it as Gamay Beaujolais rather than as Pinot Noir.*

*California Pinot Noir's comeback was sparked in the late '70s with the rediscovery of the potential of Carneros. Tchelistcheff's delicious 1946 Pinot Noir had proven the potential of Carneros's cool climate thirty years previously. Now, Acacia and Carneros Creek led the way in Carneros's experimenting with Pinot Noir. Simultaneously, Richard Sanford and Michael Benedict were exploring the grape's potential in Santa Barbara's cool climate, and the Rochiolis were planting it in the even cooler Russian River Valley of Sonoma County. Soon, other vintners and winemakers clued into the grape's potential in cool-climate vineyards and began making Pinot Noir.*

*Today, Californian Pinot Noir is righteous juice, chock-full of fragrant aromas, incredible textures, and hedonistic pleasures. And it tastes great too. It is the anti-Cabernet, fun and flexible, sex in a glass, the perfect restaurant wine thanks to its affinity with food and its wanton appeal to the senses. No wonder everyone wants more.*

*Michael Bonadies*

ide is produced. Since extraction depends on interaction with the skins, only minimal extraction can occur if the skins remain on top of the juice. The cap is moistened and mixed back into the juice by:

- pumping the juice from the bottom of the tank back over the cap, breaking it up, and forcing it back down into the juice.
- manually breaking up and punching the cap back down into the juice.
- trapping the cap at a certain level within the juice and not allowing it to rise.
- allowing the cap to remain at the top of the juice but continually spraying it with juice.

*Your Call:* You opt for pumping the juice over the cap to attain the highest degree of extraction. Since you are not content with the degree of extraction achieved through fermentation and you want a more accessible wine with more integrated tannins, you allow a period of extended maceration as well.


## Decision #2: Aging Vessel

Making an ambitious Cabernet Sauvignon calls for barrel aging, so:

1. Are you going to use French or American oak barrels or a mixture of both?
2. What percentage of new barrels will you buy?
3. Will you opt for a light, medium, or heavy char for the barrels?
4. How long will the wine age in wood?

*Your Call*

1. Sixty-forty in favor of the good old U.S. of A. There have been tremendous strides in the quality of American oak barrels, and you like what you've tasted of Cabernet Sauvignons aged with a predominance of American oak. And it doesn't hurt that the price is right: $300 for American barrels versus $600 for French.
2. 100% new barrels.
3. Split the new barrels right down the middle: Half get a medium char and half get a heavy char. You want that sexy, smokey, new oak thing going on.
4. Twenty-four months in the barrel.


## Decision #3: Play It Safe or Bet the Ranch?

Do you risk fermenting the wine with wild yeast and then releasing the finished product unfined and unfiltered?

*Your Call:* No way. You don't have an acting career to fall back on if something goes wrong. And that banker you dealt with didn't seem like the patient, sympathetic type. You go with a strain of cultured yeast, rack, fine, and lightly filter.

### Decision #4: Blending

Cabernet Sauvignon is normally blended in order to make it a more accessible wine as well as to add complexity. Merlot helps tame it by contributing softer tannins, a more velvety mouth-feel, and other fruit flavors. Cabernet Franc adds spiciness and more intense aromas. Cabernet Sauvignon is often added to a Merlot-based wine to give it more structure and tannin.

Blending may also be done between different Cabernet Sauvignon vineyards in order to lend each vineyard's unique aromas, specific flavor profile, or texture to the finished wine. And blending is the key to proprietary or Meritage wines, in which no one single variety comprises 75% of the total and the goal is a consistent style from vintage to vintage.

*Your Call:* Taste is the final judge. You may try hundreds of blends until you settle on the best one.

# MARKETING—MORE DECISIONS

While it wasn't quite the vintage of the century, the final blend tastes damn good. Who needs Hollywood?

### Decision #1—Give It a Name

You've already decided to bottle the single vineyard under your Sidecar Cellars label as the Ranch Vineyard Cabernet Sauvignon.

### Decision #2—The Label

While the Pinot Noir will be bottled with the same label you're using for your Chardonnays, you want a slightly different label for the Ranch Vineyard Cabernet Sauvignon—one that depicts a new motorcycle and sidecar speeding through the actual vineyard.

# TANNINS

*Tannins are a group of compounds that exist in many fruits and trees. You experience tannin as a bitter or astringent taste in young red wines or very strong tea. Tannins in red wine are extracted from the skins as well as from the oak barrels used in aging. They lend structure and backbone to red wine, and their antioxidant properties act as a preservative crucial to a wine's ability to age gracefully. The key with tannins is to extract them in sufficient quantities to ensure graceful aging without excessive astringency.*

## Decision #3—Price

Right now your straight Carneros Chardonnay is selling for $28 a bottle retail and your Soft Tail Vineyard Chardonnay is going for $35. You peg the Ranch Vineyard Cabernet Sauvignon at $45 and pray for high scores.

## Decision #4—Distribution

Having fired your agent (actually he dropped you first), you have had it with middlemen. And that means distributors too. However, there are ways around the three-tier system:

1. You build a tasting room in order to sell directly to tourists and visitors. Selling at retail, without anyone taking a cut in the middle, boosts your profit margin.
2. You begin offering wine for sale via a mailing list and the Internet. Again, there's no middleman and your profit margin looks even better.

## Decision #5—Marketing Plan

Thanks to the incredible success of your Chardonnay, you're a Player now. Everyone who wants your Chardonnay—distributors, restaurants, retailers, charity auctions—has to play along and take the Cabernet Sauvignon as well. You know that will alienate some people, but no more Mr. Nice Guy. The wine writers to whom you have given sneak tastes of your Ranch Vineyard Cabernet Sauvignon went gaga over it. High scores look like a lock.

## Decision #6—The Allocation Game

While you've managed to allocate more wine to the Cleveland area, the rest of the country is angry that they can't get enough of your wines, especially after all your recent releases scored 96+ and *Wine & Spirits* and the *Wine Spectator* both ran profiles of you and your winery.

# HOW TO TASTE AND APPRECIATE RED WINE

Red wines have more intense aromas and flavors, as well as more complexly layered bottle bouquets, than whites. This is what makes them more fun and interesting to taste, drink, and enjoy. On the other hand, red wines are higher in alcohol and tannins, which can make them more difficult for the budding wine lover to taste and appreciate. You could say red wine is an acquired taste.

If you haven't yet acquired that taste but are curious, start with light, fruity reds that are low in tannins and acidity, and slowly work your way up to the more complex and powerful wines. Don't forget to take notes. A few years from now, in the process of moving, you might stumble on your first red wine tasting notebook, thumb through it, and discover your one-word description for what is now your favorite red wine: "Yuck!" Tastes change and mature. Don't shut yourself off from the enjoyment of red wines because you didn't like them the first few times you tried. Give them another try. You may be surprised.

## The Differences in Tasting Reds

1.  There's more going on aromatically and flavorwise in red wines; thus there's more to discover and describe.

2.  Red wines cry out for food. When tasting tannic reds, it is important to remember that food, particularly protein, greatly lessens the effect of tannin on your tongue. So don't get too hung up on tannin and its puckering effect when tasting red wine without food.

3.  Red wines are usually higher in alcohol, which can lead to a fatigue factor not normally encountered with whites. Sniff and sip slowly as you taste to lessen the effect of the alcohol. Don't forget to spit.

4.  Color. With their deeper colors, it is necessary to tilt your glass and examine the edges of red wines to determine color and clarity.

## Do Red Wines Age?

Definitely!

# FRENCH VERSUS AMERICAN OAK

*Oak barrel aging is a given for premium red wine. With the exception of Pinot Noir, which is aged exclusively in French barrels, the question then becomes whether to use French or American oak, or both?*

1. *Track record*
   - *French oak has been harvested for centuries. Five specific forests are renowned for their barrels and the varieties they age best.*
   - *Until recently, American oak was coopered primarily for the bourbon industry and for Spanish and Australian winemakers. Today, American oak is being used more frequently for wine barrels in California.*

2. *The variables*
   - *species of oak*
   - *site of origin*
   - *curing*
   - *toasting time and temperature*

*These variables determine the "taste" of the barrel. French and American oak are decidedly different in terms of species of oak and site of origin but can be nearly identical in curing and in toasting time and temperature. The curing (or the drying of the oak prior to coopering) and the toasting of the inside of the barrel are techniques that can be duplicated in the United States. Winemakers are finding that American barrels made using French techniques for curing and toasting are very competitive with the French barrels in terms of quality.*

3. *Taste or flavor*
   - *French oak tends to contribute more complex flavors of toast, cedar, mint, and vanilla, and lends an intriguing perfume.*
   - *American oak provides a more flamboyant and obvious expression of oak, with vanilla's underlying sweetness the predominate flavor.*

4. *Price*
   - *French barrels—$600*
   - *American barrels—$300*

## But Do Red Wines Taste Better Old?

Well . . . maybe. The question is how old? There's a big difference between being old and being dead. Our fascination with very old red wines is inherited from the British, whose wine writers have had the most influence on American wine writers and thus, indirectly, on American wine drinkers. The problem is that the British worship the dead. They are raving necrophiliacs, obsessed with wines so old and tired that they're already in the grave and devoid of any sensual pleasure. Isn't pleasure what wine is supposed to be all about?

Old wines—at least the cadavers many British enjoy—are by definition elitist. Why?

1. Tasting or drinking these wines is, as a general rule, a rational or intellectual experience as opposed to a sensual one. Old wines are not known for lots of fruit, flavor, and pleasure.
2. It takes luck or lots of money (or years and years of patience as they sit down in your cellar) to "enjoy" the experience of these old wines.
3. Because these old wines command such high prices, their younger versions become commodities to be purchased and hoarded instead of being popped open and enjoyed.
4. Value. These old wines are so expensive that the experience of drinking them rarely if ever measures up to expectations.

Well-made red wines improve with bottle age as they take on added complexity and shed tannin. Most serious reds reach their peak soon after their tenth birthday, hold it for maybe another five to ten years, and then start a slow decline. The great risk in waiting for reds to reach their peak is that you may miss it. Ooops, there it goes. Gone forever and ever and ever. So buy a case of an age-worthy red and drink it over a ten- to fifteen-year period to see how the wine evolves. However, the overwhelming majority of reds produced today are meant to be consumed soon after release. Even those reds made with aging in mind are increasingly vinified in a friendlier style, one that can be enjoyed when they are in their youth as well as after they have put on a few years.

# THE MARRIAGE OF TWO VINEYARDS

*Since 1990, the Las Rocas Vineyard in the Stag's Leap District and the Manley Lane Vineyard on the Rutherford Bench have been the heart and soul of Joseph Phelps's Insignia. The blending of the fruit from these vineyards "results in a whole greater than the sum of the parts," says Craig Williams, winemaker at Joseph Phelps. "Each vineyard has its own distinctive soil and growing conditions, which result in very distinctive wines. But in blending them we end up with an even more distinctive wine."*

*Las Rocas ("The Rocks") contributes "great color and aromas," says Williams. "The wine is soft and elegant, almost feminine, with rich berry and cassis flavors." Manley Lane is a warmer site than Las Rocas, and its tremendous concentration of flavor and tannin challenge Williams's ability to tame them in a blend. "Manley fruit is heavy-duty," he says, "big, muscular, and racy, with aromas of black currant, mint, cedar, and spice. Its strength is in its tannins. It is definitely the foundation of any blend."*

*Blending Las Rocas and Manley Lane results in a balanced wine with "wild and racy aromas, lots of concentrated flavor, and firm but approachable tannin." Williams has discovered that blending the two vineyards early in the winemaking process results in a superior wine. "Blending early," he says, "enables them to grow up together. The blending is more difficult, though, because I'm judging wines that are not fully formed. But it pays off because early blending lends stability to the wine and requires less intervention. It's like soup. It always tastes better the day after it is made, as the flavors have time to marry."*

# MAJOR RED WINE GRAPE VARIETIES

### Cabernet Sauvignon

*In the Vineyard:* Easy to grow and harvest. Excellent resistance to most pests, diseases, and rain damage. A late ripener, causing problems in cool autumns.

*History:* Primary grape in the famous wines of Bordeaux as well as the premium reds of California. California clearly looks to Bordeaux as its model.

*As a Wine:* Famous! Long-lived, but can be dense and even bitterly tannic in its youth. Consequently, it is often blended with "softer" varieties such as Merlot and Cabernet Franc. It benefits from oak as well as bottle aging.

*Aromas and Flavors:* Anise, blackberry, black currant, black olive, cassis, cedar, chocolate, eucalyptus, mint, raspberry, and tobacco.

*Styles:* Big, rich, and complex, with noticeable tannins and layers of flavor.

*Food Pairing:* A tannic young Cabernet Sauvignon begs for a big steak to neutralize its aggressive tannins. Older Cabernets may be matched with more subtle lamb and beef preparations, grilled swordfish, or tuna in a red wine sauce.

*Top Producers:* Beaulieu, Beringer, Caymus, Chateau Montelena, Corison, Jordan, Joseph Phelps, La Jota, Laurel Glen, Mondavi, Shafer, Silver Oak, Spottswoode, Whitehall Lane.

*Personality:* Big man on campus.

## Merlot

*In the Vineyard:* Buds early, making frost a threat. Thin-skinned, it is susceptible to rot and is a favorite of birds (Merlot means "little blackbird"). But it ripens early, making it a good counterbet to the late-ripening Cabernet Sauvignon, especially in Bordeaux.

*History:* The grape of St. Émilion and Pomerol in Bordeaux, with Château Pétrus being the best-known producer. Traditionally a blending grape, it has on its own become the hottest red variety in the United States, increasing by 30% per year in sales.

*As a Wine:* Think of it as a softer, friendlier Cabernet Sauvignon. Lower in tannins and with very accessible fruit, Merlot is often described as supple and aromatic, with a velvety texture.

*Aromas and Flavors:* Blackberry, cassis, cherry, chocolate, mint, plum, and spice.

*Styles:* Lighter and more accessible in wines intended for immediate drinking; richer and more tannic in those built to age.

*Food Pairing:* Goes with nearly everything. Merlot may not work with lighter fish preparations.

*Top Producers:* Beringer, Clos du Bois, Duckhorn, Markham, Matanzas Creek, Newton, Pahlmeyer, St. Francis, Shafer.

*Personality:* Elected "Most Likely to Succeed."

## Pinot Noir

**In the Vineyard:** Very difficult to grow, yet prefers cooler climates. Genetically unstable, it mutates easily (there are over a thousand different clones in Burgundy alone) and is very susceptible to rot and viruses. Controlling the yield is one key to quality.

**History:** One of the oldest varieties and perhaps one of the first domesticated. It has been cultivated in Burgundy for over two thousand years.

**As a Wine:** Sublime yet frustrating, it lacks the clearly recognizable flavor traits or styles that most other grapes possess. Difficult to grow and make.

**Aromas and Flavors:** Anise, black cherry, clove, floral, raspberry, smokey, strawberry, and tea. And with age: Autumn leaves, truffles, and violet.

**Styles:** Too many to list. Best as a highly aromatic wine with a seductive texture and great length of flavor.

**Food Pairing:** Extremely versatile because of its silky texture and spicy, cherry-like flavors. Best with game birds, fowl, turkey, venison, lamb, rabbit, and heavier fish dishes. Also good with foie gras and stews using Pinot Noir as an ingredient.

**Top Producers:** Au Bon Climat, Beaulieu (a great value), Byron, Calera, Dehlinger, Etude, Gary Farrell, Hanzell, Rochioli, Sanford, Robert Sinskey, W. H. Smith, Williams Seylem, Talley.

**Personality:** A heartbreaker.

## Zinfandel

**In the Vineyard:** Prefers cool climate sites with lots of sun. An uneven ripener that tends to raisin. Vines can live more than a hundred years and continue to produce excellent wine.

**History:** A big question mark. Its mysterious origins have led California to claim it as its own.

**As a Wine:** Confused. In California, it has been made into reds, whites, blush wines, rosés, nouveau wines, dessert wines, light-style wines, full-bodied monsters, jug wines, and sparklers. Best as a still, dry red with lots of sweet fruit flavor.

**Aromas and Flavors:** Blackberry, black pepper, "brambly," cherry, leather, plum, raspberry, smokey, spice.

**Styles:** Too many to repeat. See above.

**Food Pairing:** Because of its exuberant spicy flavors and potent alcohol, Zinfandel is best suited to barbecued dishes, spare ribs, chili, hamburgers, and Mexican and Southwestern foods.

# NOT ALL MERLOTS ARE CREATED EQUAL

*It's all a question of style and comes down to your personal taste. Do you prefer a lush, accessible Merlot or one with greater guts and glory? Markham and Matanzas Creek are two top Merlot producers with very different styles.*

*The Markham Merlot (Napa Valley) is an example of the more accessible style, with bright aromas of cherry, cassis, chocolate, spice, and mint swirling up from the glass. One sip immediately reveals lush flavors of cherry, spice, and chocolate and very soft tannins. It is a rich, round wine that delivers delicious, easy drinking.*

*On the other hand, the Matanzas Creek Merlot (Sonoma Valley) has been built to age. Its aromas are dark and brooding rather than bright: black cherry, mint, spice, vanilla, roasted meat, mushroom, and chocolate. And several sips are required before the wine reveals its concentrated flavors of black cherry, chocolate, and spice. Compared to the Markham, it is fuller-bodied and more powerful yet less accessible, with harder tannins and a more pronounced acidity.*

*Both wines offer great—but very different—drinking pleasure. Your choice, then, simply comes down to a matter of style, taste, or mood.*

**Top Producers:** Cline, De Loach, Franus, Martinelli, Peachy Canyon, Quivira, Rabbit Ridge, Rafanelli, Ravenswood, Renwood, Ridge, Rosenblum, Segeshio, Steele.
**Personality:** A cowboy.

## Syrah

**In the Vineyard:** Vineyard site and control of yield are key to quality.
**History:** It is believed to have originated in the Rhône Valley. Today it is very popular in Australia and increasingly so in California.
**As a Wine:** Dense, dark monsters not for the faint of heart.
**Aromas and Flavors:** Black fruits, black pepper, rosemary, smokey, tar, and violet.
**Styles:** Typically big and tannic, although some California versions are being made in a more accessible style for earlier drinking.
**Food Pairing:** Excels with grilled meats, especially those seasoned with rosemary. Also good with vegetable dishes that contain rosemary or black olives.

**Top Producers:** Alban, Edmunds St. John, Joseph Phelps, McDowell, Neyers, Preston, Qupé, Sean H. Thackery, Swanson.

**Personality:** Elegant and reserved, with a dark and brooding side. The Pisces of the wine world.

### Grenache

**In the Vineyard:** Thrives in the hot, dry, windy conditions of the southern Rhône Valley and California, but requires a long growing season to ripen. Susceptible to mildew and insects.

**History:** Spanish in origin, it has found welcome in southern France and California as a blending wine or as the base for rosé.

**As a Wine:** Ideal as a blending wine or a rosé because of its attractive fruit flavors, color, and soft tannins.

**Aromas and Flavors:** Floral, red berries, spice, and white pepper.

**Styles:** Soft, accessible fruit.

**Food Pairing:** Roast pork or veal. Grilled chicken or tuna.

**Top Producers:** Found in Rhône-style blends made by Bonny Doon, Edmunds St. John, Jade Mountain, Joseph Phelps, McDowell, Qupé, Sean H. Thackery.

**Personality:** Spicy and fresh.

### Blends

These are not the high-priced Meritage or proprietary wines but great-value, delicious, everyday drinking reds (and much less frequently whites). These red blends of often lesser-known varieties—Petite Sirah, Carignane, Mourvèdre, Alicante Bouschet, and Gamay—are often blends of different vintages as well. Look for the following names to deliver terrific value and great drinking: Laurel Glen's "Reds," Marietta's Old Vine Red, Niebaum-Coppola's Rosso, and any of the various cuvées from Qupé.

# ROSÉ—A BLUSHING WHITE OR A BASHFUL RED?

Rosé has gotten a bad rap: "It is not a serious wine." "It is utterly devoid of ambition." "It lacks breeding." "It is too easy to drink—you don't have to think about it." You get the idea. Rosé is unfashionable, but that is starting to change.

Sounds like fun to me, though. Rosé *is* fun. It is a wine built for pure pleasure, a hedonistic wine that asks only that you quaff it down and enjoy it.

### What Is Rosé?

Is rosé a red wine without color or a white wine with color? Somewhere in between, actually. Rosé is made when red wine grapes are permitted only enough skin contact with the juice to produce the shade of pink (from barely noticeable to deep and rich, almost red) the winemaker is after. Rosé then undergoes fermentation like any white wine, with the emphasis on preserving its appealing freshness and fruitiness.

### Styles of Rosé

Rosé can be either sweet or dry. The dry versions, with lots of aroma and flavor (strawberry, raspberry, citrus, spice, and blossoms), are very enjoyable to drink. Grenache is a popular variety to make rosé with in California and France, although everything from Cabernet Sauvignon to Pinot Noir to Zinfandel (White Zinfandel) has been used to make rosé or blush wines in California.

***Top Producers:*** Bonny Doon, Edmunds St. John, Joseph Phelps, McDowell.

### Appreciating Rosé

Think rosé on a hot, lazy summer day. It is the perfect backyard barbecue or picnic wine and a great match with light fish dishes, vegetable dishes, and mildly spicy preparations.

# CONCLUSION—A TIME TO HARVEST

The grapes have turned color and the clusters hang heavy, ripening under the warm September sun. Every afternoon you stroll through the vineyard with your winegrower and vineyard manager. Pausing to pick grapes from each block, you pop them into your mouth, noting their ripeness, flavors, and balance between acidity, sugars, and tannins. After just two days, you've already formed a mental map of your vineyards—which block will be the first to be picked, which will be the last; which will deliver the best fruit and which the worst.

Harvest begins very early before sunrise one morning. You stand and watch as the pickers fan out into the vineyard. It is going to be a great vintage—you can taste it as you sample the first harvested grapes. Right then, as the first light peeks into the valley, you're at peace. There is going to be no more kissing Hollywood's ugly butt. You've had a great career—short but sweet—and resolve to dedicate yourself from now on to making great wine. Maybe in ten years or so you'll consider a Travolta-like comeback, but for right now—to hell with it. You pick up your cellular phone, call the winery, and leave a voice mail cutting the Los Angeles allocations of all your wines by 50%, with instructions to give the extra wine to Cleveland, St. Louis, and Chicago. Then, with a smile, you pull your winemaker aside and finally accede to his pleas to lead the protest against Planet Hollywood's plans to build a winery and restaurant in the heart of Napa Valley.

# RESEARCH TOPICS

### Other Important Red Varietals

As a research project, look up and read about:

- Cabernet Franc
- Gamay
- Cinsault
- Carignane
- Petit Verdot
- Malbec
- Mourvèdre
- Dolcetto
- Nebbiolo
- Sangiovese
- Tempranillo
- Barbera
- Petite Sirah

### Important Red Wine Regions

As a research project, look up and read about:

- Burgundy and its great red wine vineyards
- Bordeaux and its famous Châteaux
- Rhône Valley

- Spain
- Italy
- Australia
- New Zealand
- Long Island
- Oregon
- Washington State
- Sonoma County
- Napa Valley
- California's Central Coast

# SUGGESTED TASTINGS

**Cabernet Sauvignon**
- French oak versus American oak
- Napa versus Sonoma versus Washington State
- Bordeaux versus California
- single vineyard versus a blend of vineyards
- 100% Cabernet versus a blend
- Cabernet versus a Meritage
- different vintages of the same wine
- California, Bordeaux, and Washington State from the same vintage

**Merlot**
- 100% Merlot versus a blend
- Merlot versus Cabernet Sauvignon
- Bordeaux versus California versus Washington State versus Long Island
- Merlot versus Pinot Noir versus Zinfandel

**Pinot Noir**
- Burgundy versus California versus Oregon
- Russian River versus Carneros versus Central Coast

- Pinot Noir versus Cabernet Sauvignon
- Pinot Noir versus Merlot
- a high percentage of new oak versus a low percentage
- single vineyard versus a blend of vineyards

## Zinfandel

- Napa Valley versus Sonoma
- single vineyard versus a blend of vineyards
- old vine Zinfandel versus a regular Zinfandel
- Zinfandel versus Cabernet Sauvignon

## Syrah

- Rhône Valley versus California versus Australia (Shiraz)
- Syrah versus Cabernet Sauvignon
- 100% Syrah versus a Rhône-style blend

## Grenache

- red wine version versus rosé
- Grenache versus Syrah
- Grenache versus Zinfandel
- Grenache versus Cabernet Sauvignon
- Rhône Valley versus Provence versus California

## A Fun Tasting

Assemble a group of California Cabernet Sauvignons from the same vintage. The vintage, at a minimum, should be at least five years old. From that very same year, assemble a selection of hit songs to play during the tasting. Research the Oscar winners, bestsellers, fads, fashions, Superbowl champions, etc., from that year. Taste the wines and see what have held up better—the wines or the songs, Oscar winners, fads, etc. I guarantee you'll be surprised. And it is even more fun if you can obtain a group of wines ten years or older.

# QUESTIONS

1. Name the ways in which the vinification of red wine differs from that of white wine:

   a)  extended skin contact

   b)  _____

   c)  _____

   d)  _____

   e)  _____

   f)  _____

2. a) Which red wine is most often blended with other wines to achieve a softer, less tannic wine?  _____

   b) What are two wines it is most frequently blended with?

   _____

3. Red wine is at its best:

   a)  with food

   b)  on a hot summer day

   c)  very, very, very old

   d)  with tons of tannin

4. Red wines tend to be more complex than white wines._____**T or F**

5. Tannins are compounds in the skins of grapes that can:

   a)  make a wine taste bitter

   b)  _____

   c)  _____

6. When is a red wine ready to drink?

   a) after it's at least fifteen years old

   b) only when paired with a big steak

   c) whenever it tastes good to you

**7.** List some characteristics of *Cabernet Sauvignon* in terms of:

Aromas and Flavors: _____

Styles: _____

**8.** List some characteristics of *Merlot* in terms of:

Aromas and Flavors: _____

Styles: _____

**9.** List some characteristics of *Pinot Noir* in terms of:

Aromas and Flavors: _____

Styles: _____

**10.** List some characteristics of *Zinfandel* in terms of:

Aromas and Flavors: _____

Styles: _____

**11.** List some characteristics of *Syrah* in terms of:

Aromas and Flavors: _____

Styles: _____

**12.** List some characteristics of *Grenache* in terms of:

Aromas and Flavors: _____

Styles: _____

**13.** Rosé is:

    a) red wine without color

    b) white wine with color

    c) fortified wine

    d) a darkly colored wine

# ANSWERS

**1.**

    b)  higher fermentation temperatures

    c)  extended maceration

    d)  longer barrel aging

    e)  air contact

    f)  longer bottle aging before release

**2.**

    a)  Cabernet Sauvignon

    b)  Merlot and Cabernet Franc

**3.** a

**4.** True

**5.**

    b)  help a wine age

    c)  give a wine backbone

**6.** c

**7–12.** Refer to text, pages 107 through 111.

**13.** a and b

*Michael Bonadies*

# | 6 |

# CHAMPAGNE AND SPARKLING WINE

It is early summer as you walk through the vineyard. The vines have flowered and the fruit has begun to set. It looks as if there will be a huge crop; the vines are loaded with potential clusters. A decision will have to be made to drop some fruit in order to give the vines the chance to fully ripen the remaining clusters.

As the fog rolls in, you return home caked with dust and open your refrigerator. There's something wrong—it's filled with beer, Chardonnay, and a lone bottle of rosé. There is not a single bottle of sparkling wine to be found anywhere. And there hasn't been any for months. Has your romantic life been that much of an afterthought, with all your time and energy going into the winery? Guess so.

You jump back into your pickup and head into town. Before you know it, you're walking out of the wineshop with a mixed case of sparkling wine, intent on making room in your refrigerator for the wine of romance in hopes of improving your luck.

## THE TOP TEN REASONS TO BUY THE WINE WITH BUBBLES

1. Love
2. Sex
3. Success
4. Luxury

5. Elegance

6. Sophistication

7. A wedding or anniversary

8. New Year's Eve

9. To make a toast

10. Just because

# A MONTH LATER

You don't miss Hollywood at all. As a matter of fact, you actually enjoy working for a living, but if only that sparkling wine would work its magic. You're still waking up alone, dreaming of that special someone and making coffee for one. You take consolation in the fact that your wines are selling great and your very first Pinot Noir is awesome. You want to make more, but there are no more potential vineyard sites on your property.

**You want to make more Pinot Noir. But where?**

- Russian River. The hot spot for Pinot Noir and an hour drive away. *(Move 6 spaces.)*
- Carneros. It's your backyard. You've got a feel for it, and you like being a local. *(Advance directly to Go and collect $200.)*
- Sonoma Coast. The newest region for Pinot Noir. Promising but not yet a lock. *(Lose a turn.)*
- Santa Barbara. Produces great Pinot Noir but is too close to Los Angeles. *(Go directly to Jail. Do not pass Go.)*

**It's the Russian River or Carneros for you. What's for sale?**

- Russian River. Not much. There's only a phylloxera-infested Sauvignon Blanc vineyard on the market that could be replanted to Pinot Noir.
- Carneros. Bingo. One of the French Champagne companies has put its American sparkling wine operation up for sale. The winery and vineyards are located right over the next hill from your place. The only problem is that it's the entire operation or nothing. You had hoped just to cherry-pick its two excellent Pinot Noir vineyards.

The question is: Do you really want to make sparkling wine?

**Option I**

1. Buy the entire operation.
2. Learn to make and market sparkling wine.
3. Maybe 15,000 cases of sparkling wine will work better than one bottle in the fridge.
4. Trade in the pickup for a Porsche.

# OR

**Option II**

1. Buy the entire operation.
2. Pass on making sparkling wine and sell off everything but the Pinot Noir vineyards and one awesome Chardonnay vineyard.
3. Maybe in your case Pinot Noir works better than bubbles.
4. Trade in the pickup for a Suburban.

### The Pros and Cons

The question is, do you want to plunge into the sparkling wine business?

*Pros:* You don't know squat about making and marketing sparkling wine, but you like the way it tastes.

*Cons:* You don't know squat about making and marketing sparkling wine, but you like the way it tastes.

# DECISIONS, DECISIONS, DECISIONS

You decide not to make any decision until you've learned more about sparkling wines and how they're made. First of all, where do the bubbles come from?

### Where Do the Bubbles Come From?

The by-products of fermentation are alcohol, carbon dioxide, and heat. The bubbles in champagne and sparkling wine are dissolved carbon dioxide gas. Carbon dioxide is allowed to escape during the fermentation of still wine, but it is trapped during the making of champagne and sparkling wine. Two fermentations are necessary to produce and capture the bubbles. The first fermentation produces a still wine. The second fermentation occurs when sugar and yeast are added to the wine inside an enclosed container (a bottle or tank). Unable to escape, the carbon dioxide gas dissolves into the wine and creates the bubbles.

## Is There Any Difference Between Champagne and Sparkling Wine?

Champagne is a sparkling wine, but not all sparkling wines are champagne. Champagne is a wine from the Champagne region of northern France, an area strictly defined by law. A sparkling wine made 10 feet outside the geographic boundary of Champagne cannot be labeled champagne. Champagne is where sparkling wines were first produced and where some of the finest sparkling wines in the world are made by the process called the *méthode champenoise.* Out of respect, the majority of the world's producers of sparkling wine call their wine with bubbles sparkling wine and *not* champagne.

Sparkling wines produced by the Transfer or Charmat methods are clearly not the equal of any champagne or premium sparkling wine made by the *méthode champenoise.* The *méthode champenoise* produces wines with far greater complexity of aroma, flavor, and texture.

## The Challenge—Capturing the Stars

Sparkling wine is the youngest of all wines. It only became a possibility with the advent of glass manufacturing in the 1600s. And even then, its discovery was an accident. Prior to its discovery, winemakers in colder regions (i.e., Champagne) often had a problem with exploding wine barrels. The cool climate prolonged the fermentation process, and if the barrels were tightly sealed, the carbon dioxide could build up enough pressure to burst the barrel. However, winelovers in Paris and London noticed that the wines from these colder regions often had a natural effervescence that they found attractive.

In the late 1600s Dom Pérignon, the cellar master of a Benedictine abbey in Champagne, "discovered" champagne. Employing corks and strong glass bottles, Dom Pérignon was able to capture more of the bubbles, and champagne was born. Legend has it that with his first sip, Dom Pérignon proclaimed that he was tasting the stars.

# THE GRAPES

Champagne is made from white and red wine grapes: Chardonnay, Pinot Noir, and Pinot Meunier. California sparkling wine is made from Chardonnay and Pinot Noir, with an occasional addition of Pinot Blanc or Pinot Meunier.

When it comes to making champagne and sparkling wine, it is important to remember that style, not varietal characteristic, is the goal. When making a still wine, you want a Chardonnay to taste like a Chardonnay and a Cabernet Sauvignon to taste like a Cabernet Sauvignon, but with sparkling wine you want the smell, taste, and texture to be the *style* of the producer.

Each grape lends its own characteristics to the style:

- Chardonnay brings elegance and crispness to a wine and the stamina for it to age. In a young sparkler, it lends notes of apple and honey, and with age it brings on a nuttiness.
- Pinot Noir delivers fruit flavors and aromas and provides the body.
- Pinot Meunier contributes a spiciness and roundness.

# FARMING PRACTICES

The major difference between farming grapes for bubbles and for still wines is that sparkling wine grapes are picked at lower sugar and higher acid levels than is normal for still wines. The reasons for this are: 1) additional sugar will be added to start the second fermentation (if the grapes were picked at normal harvest sugar levels, the resulting wine would be too high in alcohol); 2) a lively, fresh acidity is an important characteristic of a high-quality sparkling wine; and 3) varietal aroma and flavor characteristics (which come with more mature fruit) are not desirable.

# HOW TO CAPTURE THE BUBBLES

There are three ways to capture the bubbles that define the specialness and elegance of sparkling wine and champagne: 1) the *méthode champenoise,* 2) the transfer method, and 3) the Charmat method.

### The *Méthode Champenoise*
The *méthode champenoise* is the process during which the secondary fermentation takes place in the bottle—the same bottle you will buy and open. It is how all champagnes and

high-quality sparkling wines are made. The *méthode champenoise* is an expensive and time-consuming process that involves the following steps:

1. *Pressing.* Whole grape clusters are gently pressed to avoid the extraction of any color or tannin. The trick here is to press the red wine grapes so that only white juice, free of any color, is obtained. The free-run juice (the first juice out of the press) is the most prized.

2. *Fermentation.* The first fermentation takes place in stainless-steel tanks. The resulting still wine is called a base wine. Base wines are kept separate until it is time to assemble the final blend, or cuvée.

3. *Blending.* The winemaker's goal with sparkling wine is to achieve a house style that will remain consistent from vintage to vintage. This is achieved through the careful blending of base wines and, when making nonvintage wines, the judicious addition of reserve wines (older base wines from earlier vintages). The result of blending is a final cuvée that the winemaker knows from experience will—after the second fermentation and several years of aging with the yeast in the bottle—result in a sparkling wine in the house style.

4. *Liqueur de tirage.* Once the cuvée has been blended, the wine is bottled. The winemaker then adds the *liqueur de tirage* (a blend of sugar, yeast, and wine) to start the second fermentation, and the bottle is sealed with a metal bottle cap.

5. *Second fermentation.* This is when the bubbles are born. During this fermentation, the carbon dioxide gas is trapped inside the bottle. As the wine ages, the gas slowly dissolves into the wine and remains trapped there until the wine is opened and its bubbles fill a glass.

6. *Lees contact.* The wine is allowed to rest on the lees *(sur lie)* for two to four years. This contact with the dead yeast cells results in added complexity and flavor.

7. *Riddling.* The dead yeast cells must be removed or the wine will be cloudy. The first step is riddling. The bottles are placed in A-frame racks. Over a period of weeks, the bottles are continually turned by hand or machine. With each slight turn, the bottle is tipped farther downward. At the end of the process, each bottle is nearly upside down and all the yeast has fallen into the neck of the bottle.

8. *Disgorging.* The bottles are first chilled to prevent any loss of carbon dioxide. They are then turned completely upside down and their necks submerged in a freezing brine bath. This action freezes the sediment and a small bit of wine. The bottle is removed from the bath and tilted. As the bottle cap is popped off, the pressure inside the bottle shoots out the ice plug containing the sediment.

9. *Dosage.* A small amount of sweetened wine is added to make up for the wine lost during disgorging. The sweetness of the dosage determines the final style and relative sweetness or dryness of the finished wine. The bottle is then corked to keep the bubbles in. After an aging period of several more months, the sparkling wine is released for sale.

## The Transfer Method

The transfer method is similar to the *méthode champenoise,* with one cost-reducing short-cut. The transfer method mimics the *méthode champenoise* through the steps of blending, second fermentation, and lees contact. But in the transfer method, the expensive, labor-intensive, time-consuming step of riddling the sediment is avoided by transferring the wine from individual bottles into a large tank. There the wine is filtered to remove the yeast deposits, the dosage is added, and the wine is pumped back into the bottles and recorked.

## The Charmat Method

In the Charmat method, the still base wines are blended in pressurized tanks following the first fermentation. The *liqueur de tirage* (sugar, yeast, and wine) is added and the second fermentation begins, producing the bubbles. The wine is then filtered and bottled under pressure, preserving the bubbles. This method is also known as the bulk process.

## Why Are *Méthode Champenoise* Wines More Expensive?

It is partly due to mystique and marketing, but mostly to the fact that producers in Champagne and California who employ this process use better-quality (i.e., more expensive) grapes and costly hand labor, and are willing to carry the cost of years of bottle aging. When you taste a bottle made by the *méthode champenoise* alongside wines made by the transfer method and the Charmat method, there is no comparison in taste, flavor, complexity, and elegance.

# MARKETING AND SELLING THE BUBBLES

If you were to begin producing and selling sparkling wines, here are some marketing decisions you might make based on what you've learned so far and Sidecar Cellars' sterling reputation as a producer of excellent still wines:

### Decision #1—The Name
Retain the original brand name.

### Decision #2—The Label
Redesign the label to look more hip and add at the top of it: "Sidecar Cellars Presents:"

### Decision #3—Price
If you stick with the established brand name, you're stuck with their high-end pricing. If you decide to tackle sparkling wine, you'll have to lower the price to be more competitive.

### Decision #4—Distribution
Your distribution system is already in place, but given the competitiveness and small scale (compared to still wines) of the sparkling wine market, you will have to cut deals (i.e., "I'll give you more of my Chardonnay, Merlot, Cabernet Sauvignon, or Pinot Noir, if you take on and push my sparkling wine").

### Decision #5—Marketing Plan
1. Sell romance, love, and sex.
2. Sell celebration and holidays.
3. Sell mystique, success, luxury, elegance, and sophistication.

The first one you could do in your sleep. The second takes care of itself. The third is more interesting, and perhaps more telling, about the appeal of sparkling wine and champagne. Champagne was, and still is, the drink of royalty. The majority of Champagne's early production was reserved for the Russian czars, English and French monarchs, and countless other titled personages. The mystique of sparkling wine, thanks no doubt to this early royal connection, is a very important motivation for purchasing it. Everyone feels richer, more sophisticated, more successful, and more elegant when they order a bottle of sparkling wine. It is cheaper and quicker than therapy for boosting self-esteem.

### Decision #6—Allocations

Not a problem. The bigger challenge will be selling everything you make.

# HOW TO TASTE AND APPRECIATE CHAMPAGNE AND SPARKLING WINE

When tasting sparkling wines, it is important to remember that you are entering a new world—and a very different world from that of still wines. This wonderful new world is one of elegance and bubbles, sophistication and stars. Sparkling wines are the seductive and mysterious members of the wine world. Consequently, a slightly different approach is required when tasting them:

## Temperature:

Sparkling wine should be served colder than white wine, but never go for the quick chill in the freezer (it can get very messy—trust me).

## Popping the Cork:

Actually you don't want to pop the cork, because that can cause the loss of precious bubbles. Free the foil and wire cage and grip the cork tightly in one hand (pointed away from any potential victims or windows). Tilt the bottle at a 45-degree angle and slowly turn it with your other hand while holding the cork steady. Just before you feel the cork about to pop, tilt it and ease it out with barely a sound.

## Glassware:

Use only fluted champagne glasses, which show the bubbles best. Avoid saucer-shaped glasses at all costs. The glasses must be clean. Any soap film or residue will kill the bubbles.

## Swirling:

Swirling is for still wines. Swirling a sparkling wine will only speed up the loss of bubbles.

## Appearance:

Bubbles, bubbles, and more bubbles. Sparkling wines are all about bubbles—without their life force, the wine doesn't sparkle, sing, or please. Look at the bubbles in the glass. They should be small and continuous.

## Color:

The wine should be clear. The color can vary from pale yellow to salmon, depending on the proportions of white and red wine grapes used in the cuvée.

## Aromas and Flavors:

Apple, butterscotch, citrus, floral, honey, lychee, melon, pear, roasted nuts, toast, and yeast.

## Top Producers:

Domaine Chandon, Iron Horse, Jordan Sparkling Wine Company, Mumm Napa Valley, Roederer Estate, Scharffenberger, Schramsberg.

## Personality:

Elegant and charming, with a hint of intrigue. A wine that always seduces, sip after sip, with its many and varied charms.

# STYLES—ELEGANCE IN A GLASS

Style, and not varietal characteristic, is the key to understanding sparkling wines. Style and elegance are synonymous in the very best sparkling wines. The Oxford English Dictionary defines elegance as "Refined grace of form and movement, tastefulness of adornment, refined luxury." The very best sparkling wines are indeed possessed of refined flavors, harmoniously graceful in their impression on the palate and tastefully luxurious in the complexity of sensual pleasures they offer, sip after sip.

What follows is a list of the various styles of champagnes and sparkling wines:

## Nonvintage:

The standard bearer of most producers' house style and the number-one style of sparkling wine produced in the world. Most often a blend with which the winemaker, year in and year out, attempts to produce a consistent and recognizable style of wine.

## Vintage:

More common in California, where favorable weather conditions produce excellent vintages year after year. Consequently, California producers are able to deliver a consistent style of sparkling wine from vintage to vintage. In Champagne, the opposite is true. Champagne is one of the most northerly wine-producing areas and experiences variable weather, which can result in great differences in grape quality from year to year. The answer in Champagne is to produce nonvintage wines through which the winemaker achieves consistency by blending wines from different vintages in order to achieve a recognizable style. To be labeled with a vintage, a California wine must be made of at least 95% grapes from the year indicated.

## Blanc de Noirs:

This is typically a sparkling wine made from Pinot Noir grapes. It can be vintage or nonvintage and often exhibits a slight pink hue in the glass.

## Blanc de Blancs:

A sparkling wine made from Chardonnay grapes. Lighter and more delicate than a blanc de noirs, it can be vintage or nonvintage.

## Rosé:

A sparkling wine with a rosé color, which is achieved by: 1) a certain portion of color extracted during the press of red wine grapes, or 2) red wine mixed in to achieve the desired color. Can be vintage or nonvintage.

## Crémant:

A Crémant from Champagne is a sparkling wine with fewer bubbles than normal. It is very rare, and most producers have stopped making it. This less fizzy version is not to be confused with Crémant d'Alsace, Crémant de Bourgogne, Crémant de Loire, etc., where the

# BUBBLES AND FOOD

*Sparkling wine is the most versatile of wines because it complements a greater range of foods, flavors, and preparations than other wines and does so with great flair. A superb sparkling wine makes everyone feel better and everything taste great. Sparkling wines pair best with light seafood, shellfish, Asian dishes, and poultry. Sparkling wines excel with sushi, sashimi, and lightly smoked foods. And sparkling wines stand on their own as the perfect aperitif, thanks to their ability to stimulate the senses and spark the appetite.*

term "Crémant" indicates a high-quality French sparkling wine produced outside the boundaries of Champagne.

## Late Disgorged or Recently Disgorged:

A sparkling wine that has aged on the lees for a longer period than is normal for a producer. Results in a more complexly flavored wine. Can be vintage or nonvintage.

## *Tête de Cuvée:*

The top-of-the-line sparkling wine from a producer. More common in France than California. No expense is spared to produce the very best sparkling wine. Can be vintage or nonvintage.

# CALIFORNIA VERSUS CHAMPAGNE—THE "TOAST" QUESTION

Ever since the resurgence of the California fine wine industry in the early 1970s, constant comparison has been made between California and French wines. The concern here is, how do California sparkling wines and French champagnes match up?

The answer is favorably. But that doesn't prevent sommeliers, winemakers, winery owners, and wine lovers from throwing up their hands and lamenting the lack of "toast or yeast" aromas and flavors in California sparklers when compared to champagnes which are decidedly toastier or yeastier in their flavor profile. Meanwhile, the French look on with amusement and chuckle, "Yeast is to make bread. Toast is for jam."

California sparkling wines are all about fruit and generosity of flavor. The French would kill to be able to work with such exuberant fruit. Toast or yeast is a predominate aroma and flavor in champagne because of the climate. Champagne is too cool for the grapes to develop an intensity of flavor comparable to California grapes. It is this intensity of fruit that makes California sparklers so special and that, at the same time, masks the toast and yeast flavors in a young wine. With bottle age, the fruit aromas recede slightly and the toast and yeast aromas become more noticeable.

| Wine | Dryness Level |
|------|---------------|
| BRUT NATURE | ABSOLUTELY DRY |
| BRUT | DRY |
| EXTRA DRY | LESS DRY |
| SEC | SLIGHTLY SWEET |
| DEMI-SEC | SWEETER |
| DOUX | SWEETEST |

# IS IT DRY?

Dry is confusing. Champagnes and sparkling wines labeled Extra Dry are not exactly "dry," because their dosage produces a wine that can best be described as less dry. Here are the levels of relative dryness for sparkling wines:

# DO CHAMPAGNES AND SPARKLING WINES AGE?

Yes and no. Drink California sparkling wines sooner rather than later. But with time, even champagnes lose their bubbles, no matter how tightly corked or well cellared.

# What If the Bubbles Disappear?

*It can happen in the best of homes. Suddenly, champagne and sparkling wine disappoints because of a lack of bubbles. If this happens, check your glasses. The problem is almost certainly due to a build-up of soap residue on the glasses, which kills the bubbles. Change your dish soap. If that doesn't work, purchase a diamond-tipped etching tool (available in art-supply stores) and make a small scratch inside the bottom of every champagne flute. This small scratch will magically bring the bubbles back to life.*

*A Word of Caution: Handle the etching tool and the champagne glasses very carefully in order not to break a glass and cut yourself.*

# YOUR DECISION ON SPARKLING WINE

You decide to buy the entire operation, but it's a big NO on making the wine with bubbles. While sparkling wine is delicious, your big NO is based on very practical decisions:

1. Its magic hasn't worked for you. The bottle of sparkling wine has been in your refrigerator for weeks now. Just think how long it would take you to get rid of an annual production of 15,000 cases.

2. The French are bailing out of California. In addition to the company you are negotiating with, another French Champagne firm is looking for a buyer for its California operation.

3. Most of the other sparkling wine producers are increasing their production of still wines—Chardonnay and Pinot Noir—while cutting back on their production of sparkling wines. Clearly, the demand for quality sparkling wines just isn't there.

4. Champagne production has tripled, and French producers are dumping product in the United States at a low price.

5. Sparkling wine costs more than still wine and is taxed more than still wine because it is considered a luxury item. The 1998 federal tax for still wine is $1.07 per gallon, and for sparkling wine, $3.40 per gallon.

6. You haven't been back to Montana and your ranch for a very long time.

# RESEARCH TOPICS

Look up and research the following topics:

- Champagne
- Dom Pérignon
- Pinot Meunier
- Spumante
- Sekt
- Charmat method
- transfer method

# SUGGESTED TASTINGS

- Champagne versus California sparklers
- *méthode champenoise* versus Charmat method versus transfer method
- different vintages of the same wine
- comparison of styles: nonvintage versus vintage versus blanc de noirs versus blanc de blancs versus rosé versus Crémant versus late disgorged versus *tête de cuvée*
- Sparkling wines with a wide variety of different foods

# QUESTIONS

1. What is the difference between champagne and sparkling wine? _____
_____
_____

**2.** What is the *méthode champenoise?* _____

_____

_____

_____

**3.** Riddling is _____

_____

_____

**4.** *Liqueur de tirage* is _____

_____

**5.** Dosage is _____

_____

_____

**6.** What is the transfer method of making sparkling wines? _____

_____

_____

_____

**7.** What is the Charmat method of making sparkling wines? _____

_____

_____

_____

**8.** What is most important in the making of sparkling wines and champagnes?
   a)  varietal character
   b)  style
   c)  vintage

**9.** The grapes for champagne and sparkling wine are picked at higher sugar levels and lower acid levels than other wines.          **T or F**

**10.** Cabernet Sauvignon is a grape used in making California sparkling wine.

**T or F**

**11.** Blanc de blancs is made with Chardonnay grapes.

**T or F**

**12.** Swirling sparkling wines dissipate the bubbles faster.

**T or F**

**13.** Drink California sparkling wines sooner rather than later.

**T or F**

**14.** Sparkling wine is one of the most versatile wines in terms of food pairings.

**T or F**

**15.** The best way to chill a sparkling wine quickly is to keep it in the freezer for more than twenty minutes.

**T or F**

**16.** What is the cuvée?
   a) the level of alcohol
   b) the final blend
   c) the amount of bubbles

**17.** If a sparkling wine loses its bubbles in the glass, the culprit is probably:
   a) the wine is perfectly chilled
   b) a scratched wineglass
   c) soap residue

**18.** To be labeled with a vintage, a California sparkling wine must be made of at least _____ % grapes from the year indicated.
   a) 95
   b) 75
   c) 65
   d) 90

# ANSWERS

1. A sparkling wine may only be called champagne if it is produced within the geographic region of Champagne.

2. It is the process in which the secondary fermentation takes place in the bottle, after which the sediment is riddled and disgorged.

3. The slow turning and tipping of the bottle until all lees sediment settles in the neck, for easier disgorging.

4. The mixture of yeast, sugar, and wine added to the bottle to start the second fermentation.

5. The small amount of sweetened wine added to make up for the wine lost during disgorging.

6. A cheaper shortcut in which, after the second fermentation, the wine is filtered in a large tank, then returned to the individual bottles.

7. A method in which the second fermentation takes place not in the bottles but in a large tank.

8. b

9. False

10. False

11. True

12. True

13. True

14. True

15. False

16. b

17. c

18. a

*Michael Bonadies*

136

# |7|

# DESSERT WINE

One day, back in Montana, you're out riding, when you meet up with your neighbor, a gorgeous cowbabe/hunky cowguy (circle the one that's to your taste), who owns the adjacent ranch. You've seen each other in town and at Ranchers Association meetings but have never spoken until now. You hit it off and make plans to get together for dinner Saturday at your place. He/she (circle one) insists on bringing dessert and a dessert wine.

## ELEVEN OTHER REASONS THAN WHAT SATURDAY NIGHT MIGHT BRING TO GET EXCITED ABOUT DESSERT WINES

1. *Botrytis cinerea*
2. California late-harvest wines
3. California ice wines
4. Sauternes
5. Château d'Yquem
6. Auslese
7. Beerenauslese
8. Trockenbeerenauslese
9. Bonnezeaux
10. Quarts de Chaume
11. The most intense taste sensation in the world of wine

# DECISIONS, DECISIONS, DECISIONS

You're out of practice, and it doesn't help that sparks flew between you—even your horses sensed it. You want to make Saturday night perfect. So, what to cook? What wines will you serve? What mood will you set?

### Decision #1: What Comes First?

Food or wine? Wine or food? Then you remember the bottle of sparkling wine standing ready in your refrigerator.

*Your Call:* Grab a beer to calm your nerves right now, and start Saturday night off with a glass of bubbles. Use the bottle of sparkling wine that's been in the refrigerator for months for cooking and bring a fresh bottle up from the cellar.

### Decision #2: Food

What are you going to cook? Beef, pasta, or fish?

*Your Call:* Beef is too heavy, too primal for a first dinner. Pasta is too L.A. Fish it is. You decide to get up early Saturday morning and go fishing for trout. Then you call the Oakville Grocery in Napa Valley to FedEx your favorite olives, mesclun greens, fresh tarragon, and baby spinach.

### Decision #3: Wine

Your wine or someone else's? You head down to your cellar.

*Your Call:* An hour and a thousand second guesses later, you emerge clutching an older vintage of your Soft Tail Vineyard Chardonnay.

### Decision #4: The Mood

You want to strike exactly the right mood: friendly, with a hint of romance but with not a whiff of desperation.

*Your Call:* Candles, but not too many. And a fire because the nights are getting chilly.

# HOW SWEET IT IS

The candles have burned down, the wax dripping on the tablecloth as you open the dessert wine your neighbor has brought over: a California late-harvest Riesling. Wow! Sweet and intensely flavored, yet refreshing, with a lively acidity and luscious flavors, it is unlike any-thing you've ever tasted, but then so is your neighbor as you kiss for the very first time. You're smitten. Both by the dessert wine and by your neighbor, who is a fellow Cleveland Indians fan!

## So you want to make a dessert wine?

Enough already with the wine! You clearly need to spend more time in Montana getting to know your neighbor better. *(Keep on passing Go and collecting $200.)*

But still, you're curious: What exactly is a dessert wine?

# WHAT EXACTLY IS A DESSERT WINE?

A dessert wine can be any of a wide variety of sweet wines used to accompany or replace dessert. And many of the world's best dessert wines are made from grapes infected by *Botry-tis cinerea*.

## What Is *Botrytis Cinerea?*

Normally, the last thing you'd ever want in your vineyard, unless you're into making dessert wines. *Botrytis cinerea* is a common blue-gray fuzzy mold that attacks grapes and other fruits and vegetables. *Botrytis* is also known by the names *Edefäule* (Germany), *pourriture noble* (France) and noble rot. Under ideal conditions, *Botrytis* infestation in a vineyard results in grapes that produce a rich, luscious, sweet white wine, golden in color, balanced in acid-ity, and bursting with intensely concentrated flavors and the aromas of honey, apricot, peach, apple, spice, and nuts.

***In the Vineyard:*** *Botrytis cinerea* is normally a grower's nightmare; its appearance can threaten the destruction of a vineyard's fruit. The sole exception is when the winemaker is hoping for the special dessert wines that *Botrytis* produces. *Botrytis* is present in most vine-yards, and its growth is encouraged by rain, high humidity, or fog. *Botrytis* attacks many parts of a grape vine, but its favorite target is the skin of ripening grapes. Under the wrong conditions—lots of rain, or rain followed by hot, humid weather—it attacks and splits open the grapes, paving the way for other molds and bacteria to ruin the crop. Under the right conditions—rain, very high humidity, or foggy mornings followed by sunny, dry afternoons—*Botrytis* spreads slowly through the vineyard. Rather than splitting the grapes, *Botrytis* now pierces hundreds of tiny holes in their skins. The holes allow water to evaporate from the infected grapes. This process of dehydration greatly concentrates the flavor and sugar of the grapes.

**Harvest:** *Botrytis* does not equally infect the grapes in a single cluster, let alone infect an entire vineyard. Consequently, the harvest of botrytised fruit (harvested at a sugar level approximately twice that of dry table wines) usually takes place over a period of one or two weeks. Each morning the pickers sweep through the vineyard and harvest the infected grapes one by one.

**In the Winery:** When the *Botrytis*-affected grapes arrive at the winery, they are treated differently from healthy grapes. The challenge is to press as much juice as possible from grapes that are well on their way to becoming raisins. The combination of a very high sugar level and dehydration results in a "juice" that is closer to the consistency of honey than freshly squeezed fruit juice.

The high sugar level also acts as a natural preservative that is inhospitable to most yeast. Special strains of yeast that can survive and multiply in a high sugar environment must be employed in order to achieve a successful fermentation.

**The Result:** A rich, luscious wine that is high in sugar and typically lower in alcohol than table wines, with *Botrytis* adding a noticeable layer of honey-like aromas and flavors to the wine.

# THE WORLD'S GREAT DESSERT WINES

### California

The models for California dessert wines hail from Germany and Sauternes. Wineries work with Sémillon, Sauvignon Blanc, Muscat, and Riesling (and with its hybrids such as Scheurebe) grapes. While there has been some experimentation with artificially induced *Botrytis cinerea* infestations in the vineyard, most California producers take their chances with nature. California dessert wines range from sweet to very sweet, depending on harvest conditions and the style of wine the winemaker is attempting to make.

### France

**Sauternes:** A region in Bordeaux where botrytised Sémillon and Sauvignon Blanc grapes

# Praying for Rain in Sunny California

*I have to admit I was stunned when I heard Craig Williams, winemaker at Joseph Phelps Vineyards, confess that he often prays for rain during harvest. Rain?!!! The cause of rot, mildew, diluted grapes, lousy vintages, and mold—ah, mold! When I recovered from my shock, I listened to what Craig was really saying: "The problem in California is dryness. For Botrytis to flourish we need foggy, cloudy mornings. The afternoon sun is okay because it keeps the Botrytis from running rampant. But there is nothing more frustrating than to see Botrytis starting to take hold in one of our Sémillon or Riesling vineyards and then for a warm, dry spell to hit and dry it up. That's when I pray for rain. Rain in that one vineyard and nowhere else."*

*Being a dessert wine lover and a big fan of the sweet wines Craig produces at Joseph Phelps Vineyards, I no longer envy California's sunny weather. I now have a marvelous mental image that comes to me every fall as harvest approaches: a small rain cloud hovering over Craig's head as he locks wills with Mother Nature—will she be kind enough to grant his wish for Botrytis this year?*

produce great sweet wines. The blend is typically 80% Sémillon and 20% Sauvignon Blanc, and the wine is aged in oak barrels. Château d'Yquem is considered by many to be the greatest dessert wine in the world.

**Barsac:** A neighboring region of Sauternes that produces similarly styled dessert wines.

**Loire Valley:** The dessert wines of the Loire Valley—Vouvray, Bonnezeaux, and Quarts de Chaume—are made from botrytised Chenin Blanc grapes.

## Germany

Riesling is king. Allowed to ripen late into the fall, Riesling attains high sugar levels without losing its crisp acidity. *Botrytis* is less common in the vineyards of Germany because of weather conditions, and as a result, botrytised Rieslings are very rare and highly prized.

The following are the gradations of dessert wine Rieslings produced in Germany listed from sweet to sweetest:

**Auslese:** Wine made from very ripe, handpicked clusters.

**Beerenauslese:** Wine made from hand-picked grapes that are very ripe and often botrytised.

**Trockenbeerenauslese:** Wine made from handpicked shriveled grapes that are *Botrytis-*affected.

# TRUE LOVE

You spend the next Saturday night at your neighbor's, watching the Indians game via satellite TV. It is perfect: hot dogs, peanuts, and a chilled rosé. You're in love and think it will last.

# DO DESSERT WINES LAST?

Definitely! The very best ones, thanks to their high sugar and acidity, can last for many years.

# HOW TO TASTE AND APPRECIATE DESSERT WINE

Dessert wines are not for the timid or shy. Their intensity of flavor, richness of texture, and level of sweetness are the basis for sensual pleasures unsurpassed in the world of wine. And because of their power and concentration, dessert wines demand your total attention when tasting them.

## Temperature:

Serve slightly colder than you would a white wine.

## Glassware:

A small glass, often called a port glass, works best. Because of dessert wine's concentration and intensity, a small serving will suffice.

## Half Bottles:

A half bottle will serve six people.

## Appearance and Color:

Often a deep golden color, it can darken and take on reddish tones with age.

## Aromas and Flavors:

Vary slightly depending on the varietal used, but high-quality dessert wines typically exhibit intense aromas and flavors of apricot, honey, nuts, peach, and spice.

## Food Pairing:

The classic pairing for Sauternes is foie gras or Roquefort cheese, but the most common pairing is with dessert. Try to avoid super-sweet desserts as well as desserts with tons of citrus, both of which will negatively affect your perception of the wine's pleasure. And be careful of chocolate-based desserts; they can be tricky. You're best off with fruit- and nut-based desserts of medium sweetness or skipping dessert altogether and just enjoying a glass of dessert wine instead.

## Top Producers:

Bonny Doon, De Loach, Far Niente, Ferrari-Carano, Il Podere dell' Olivos, Joseph Phelps, Mondavi, Navarro.

# CRYOEXTRACTION, OR WHAT'S IN THE FREEZER?

*Eiswein, or ice wine, is an extremely rare form of dessert wine. It occurs only when grapes are left on the vines in the hope of an early freeze. Once frozen, the grapes are picked immediately and pressed while still frozen. Freezing acts similarly to* **Botrytis cinerea.** *While* **Botrytis** *causes the grapes to lose water via evaporation, freezing locks the water up in ice and concentrates the sugar and flavor components in what little liquid remains. Pressing frozen grapes is like pressing a block of ice— it must be done very slowly and carefully in order not to damage the press.*

*Cryoextraction is the process that allows winemakers to artificially mimic nature in the production of ice wines. In cryoextraction, ripe grapes are harvested, immediately frozen, and kept in the freezer until the harvest is over and the press is freed up. The grapes are then trucked to the winery and pressed. By law, a cryoextracted wine cannot be labeled ice wine or* **Eiswein,** *which leads to creative names like "Eis" or "Vin du Glacière." However, the quality of cryoextracted wines is such that it is often impossible to differentiate them from the real thing.*

**Personality:**

Intense and focused and very, very rare. Demanding.

# DESSERT WINES—DECISIONS

You could care less about making or marketing dessert wines, as you are spending more and more time in Montana. And when you're back in wine country, you spend all your time daydreaming about riding off into the sunset with your true love.

# RESEARCH TOPICS

Look up and research the following:

- Sauternes
- Barsac
- Vouvray
- Bonnezeaux
- Quarts de Chaume
- *Botrytis cinerea*
- Auslese
- Beerenauslese
- Trockenbeerenauslese
- *Eiswein*
- Muscat
- fortified wines

# SUGGESTED TASTINGS

- Sauternes versus California dessert-style Sémillon or Sauvignon Blanc
- Auslese versus Beerenauslese versus Trockenbeerenauslese

- comparison of dessert-style wines of similar sweetness from France, Germany, and California
- California dessert-style Sémillon versus California dessert-style Riesling
- a true *Eiswein* versus a cryoextracted ice wine
- botrytised dessert wine versus a nonbotrytised dessert wine

# QUESTIONS

1. What is noble rot? _____

_____

_____

2. To ferment the thick juice from botrytised grapes, special strains of _____ are employed that can survive and multiply in a high _____ environment.

3. Sauternes is a region in _____ where botrytised _____ and _____ produce great sweet wines.

4. The typical blend of Sémillon and Sauvignon Blanc in a Sauternes is:
   a) 50% Sémillon, 50% Sauvignon Blanc
   b) 25% Sémillon, 75% Sauvignon Blanc
   c) 95% Sémillon, 5% Sauvignon Blanc
   d) 80% Sémillon, 20% Sauvignon Blanc

5. Name the grape that makes the famous sweet wines of Germany:

_____

6. Describe the grapes used for a Beerenauslese wine: _____

_____

_____

**7.** Name four grapes that California winemakers employ to produce dessert-style wines:

    a) <u>Riesling</u>

    b) _____

    c) _____

    d) _____

**8.** Acidity and_____ ensure a premium dessert wine's ability to age.

**9.** _____ is one of the rarest dessert wines. How is it produced? _____

_____

_____

_____

**10.** Explain the process of cryoextraction: _____

_____

_____

_____

**11.** Dessert wines should be served colder than white wines.  **T or F**

**12.** *Botrytis cinerea* thrives in hot, dry weather.  **T or F**

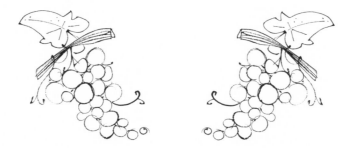

# ANSWERS

1. Noble rot is another name for *Botrytis cinerea,* a mold that under ideal conditions produces great dessert-style wines.

2. yeast; sugar

3. France; Sémillon and Sauvignon Blanc

4. d

5. Riesling

6. Beerenauslese is a wine made from handpicked grapes that are very ripe and often botrytised.

7. b) Sémillon

   c) Sauvignon Blanc

   d) Muscat

8. A high level of residual sugar.

9. *Eiswein. Eiswein* is produced when grapes left on the vines freeze. Picked immediately and pressed while still frozen, the grapes produce an intensely sweet and flavored juice.

10. Cryoextraction is an artifical method of making ice wines. The grapes are frozen in a commercial freezer and then pressed.

11. True

12. False

# | 8 |

# HISTORY, THE LAW, AND HEALTH

*"In vino veritas."*

Before you and your true love can ride off into the sunset, the long arm of the law lunges for your throat. A certain Sunbelt state has issued a felony indictment against you for direct-shipping wine into the state to a mail-order customer. Fueled by your "reborn" celebrity, all hell breaks loose as the neo-Prohibitionists seize their chance and begin picketing video stores renting your movies. Just when you thought the publicity couldn't get any worse, the attorney general for the Sunbelt state goes on national TV claiming that the bulk of your direct wine shipments to his state have been to underage drinkers (yeah, right, at $375+ a case). Welcome to wine and the law. And you thought Hollywood was a vipers' nest.

## AT THE BEGINNING

According to Genesis, God created the world in six days, resting on the seventh. Did He drink wine or beer as He sat in His BarcaLounger watching NFL football?

It's unlikely it was either, since Adam got tossed out of the Garden of Eden for eating a politically correct apple, not for getting hammered on applejack.

Noah gets credit, post-flood, for being the first to make wine, as well as for the first good buzz in the Old Testament. The fact that Noah lived to the ripe old age of 950 is an inspiring example of wine's health benefits. But the first wine-inspired hangover (and its cure) certainly predate the writing of the Bible by thousands of years. One of our ancient ancestors—*Homo erectus,* Neanderthal man, Cro-Magnon man, or perhaps an early *Homo sapiens*—one day accidentally discovered that fermented grapes or grape juice took the edge off a rough day of being chased by woolly mammoths and saber-toothed tigers and overindulged. Of course, there was a price to pay the next morning, but the drink was certainly worth the pain.

# WINE IN THE ANCIENT WORLD

Civilizations since the beginning of time have wrestled with mixed feelings regarding wine's power to incite ecstasy or misery, happiness or sadness, mellowness or violence. For the early Egyptians, Greeks, Hebrews, and Romans, wine was a civilizing force when viewed as a part of religion, as a dietary staple, and as a key trade item. When abused, it was seen as a threat to society. It was a gift from the gods, but not one without its own headaches. Consequently, it is not surprising that each of these ancient civilizations tried to harness the supernatural power of the grape through religion and ritual.

The Egyptians, who planted extensive vineyards, restricted wine drinking to the gods, royalty, the priesthood, and other members of the ruling class. The rabble who built the pyramids had to make do with beer.

For the Hebrews, once they made their getaway thanks to Moses and his neat trick of parting the Red Sea, wine represented prosperity and merited numerous mentions in the Old Testament. Except for the slight disapproval expressed over Noah's first bender (and Biblical experts are divided on the exact interpretation of that passage), the majority of wine's appearances in the Bible are favorable, i.e., "wine that maketh glad the heart of man," Psalms 104:15. And because wine was a symbol of prosperity, even more so than milk and honey, it was a fitting sacrifice to God.

The Greeks not only helped spread viticulture and winemaking around the Mediterranean, they also covered all the angles. Wine, which was part of the everyday diet, was also used in religious ceremonies, drunk at feasts, prescribed as medicine, traded all over the known world in amphorae, and featured at the symposia where men gathered for conversation and drinking games. Wine was also essential to the worship of Dionysus, the god of wine, and to his followers' ritual drunkenness. The Greek Dionysus—better known as the Roman Bacchus (a chubby, good-natured, curly-headed dude)—and his followers' violent and uncontrolled revelries were viewed by many Greeks as subversive threats to society's reason and order.

# RESPONSIBLE CONSUMPTION

*"And Noah began to be a husbandman, and he planted a vineyard: And he drank of the wine and was drunken, and he was uncovered within his tent" (Genesis 9:20–21). Where there's alcohol, there's drunkenness. And where there's drunkenness, there's disapproval. And that's basically what happened to the three-martini lunch.*

The wines of ancient times, in some cases made from the same variety in existence today, were very different. The Greeks and Romans cut their wine with water, sometimes even with seawater. Only barbarians drank wine straight. The Greeks favored wines flavored with resins (thanks to the resin used to seal amphorae), herbs, perfume, and honey. The Romans were partial to smoked wines and wines boiled in lead vessels (talk about bad vintages) to concentrate the flavor. The Romans expanded viticulture and winemaking throughout their Empire, giving birth to what are today some of the best vineyard regions in France, Germany, and Spain. The Romans also gave birth to the first wine critics, as Virgil, Horace, and Pliny the Elder held forth eloquently on individual wines, regions, vintages, and winemaking techniques. The Romans were also among the first to use wooden barrels to store and age wine.

# WINE IN THE MEDIEVAL WORLD

Wine reached its height of religious significance with the birth of Christianity. Not only was Christ's transformation of water into wine at the wedding feast at Cana his first miracle, but his words at the Last Supper, as he picked up his wine cup, sealed wine's symbolic importance to Christianity's central mystery: "And as they were eating, Jesus took bread, and blessed it, and brake it, and gave it to the disciples, and said, Take, eat; this is my body. And he took the cup, and gave thanks, and gave it to them, saying, Drink ye all of it; For this is my blood of the new testament, which is shed for many for the remission of sins" (Matthew 26:26–28).

Wine is required for Christians to celebrate the sacrament of the Eucharist, which reenacts the Last Supper, transforming the bread and wine into the body and blood of Christ. Viticulture and winemaking thus became very important to Christian societies, but especially to the monastic communities that proliferated during the Middle Ages.

If the Roman Catholic Church was the keeper of knowledge during the Dark Ages, then its great monastic orders—the Benedictines, Carthusians, and Cistercians—were the keepers of winegrowing and winemaking knowledge. Thanks to the many gifts and grants of vineyards given by noble and wealthy individuals attempting to secure their salvation, as well as their own vineyard development, monasteries became owners of many of the most famous vineyards in Burgundy, Bordeaux, Champagne, the Loire Valley, the Rhône Valley, Spain, and Germany. As these monasteries prospered, thanks in part to their vineyards, they strove to make the best wine possible and were responsible for advancing new techniques for growing vines and making wines. Like the Greeks and Romans before them, as the monastic orders expanded their "empires" by saving souls, they also spread viticultural and winemaking knowledge throughout Europe and eventually to the New World.

# WINE IN THE NEW WORLD

The Jesuits may have gotten to the New World first, establishing vineyards in the late 1500s in what are now Chile, Argentina, and Peru. But in the late 1700s, the Franciscan friar Junípero Serra had the foresight to turn northward into California, establishing missions and vineyards as he went.

Things remained quiet on the winemaking front in California until the Gold Rush brought thousands and thousands of thirsty immigrants, who created a new market for wine.

## Meanwhile, Back East

By A.D. 1000, Leif Ericsson had already "discovered" North America and named it Vinland for the profusion of wild grape vines that grew there. Early Norse settlers may have been the first to make wine in the New World, but the early American colonists who tried making wine from the native varieties found the results very unappealing. Thomas Jefferson was only one among many colonists who attempted to grow imports of the European *Vitis vinifera* vines and failed as weather, diseases, and pests (especially phylloxera) destroyed their vineyards. A chance hybridization between a *vinifera* vine and a native *Vitis labrusca* vine paved the way for limited success. Soon there were many different hybrids. Commercial wine production sprung up in the early 1800s in Ohio, Indiana, New York, and Missouri.

### California or Bust

The Gold Rush in 1849 brought thousands of adventurers and fortune seekers to California. San Francisco's population grew nearly overnight from 850 to 85,000. One of the forty-niners was Count Agoston Haraszthy of Hungary, who founded the Buena Vista winery in Sonoma Valley in 1857. Haraszthy is credited with introducing many *Vitis vinifera* varieties to California from vine cuttings he had brought over from Europe.

Haraszthy and his winery faced stiff competition from General Mariano Vallejo, the onetime Mexican governor of California whose wines won top honors at the State Fair in 1856 and 1857, and the Bundschu family (Rhinefarm, 1858) in Sonoma; and in Napa from Charles Krug (Charles Krug Winery, 1861), Jacob Schram (Schramsberg Vineyards, 1862), Gustave Niebaum (Inglenook Vineyards, 1879), and Georges de Latour (Beaulieu Vineyards, 1899). Whether the competition was too tough or he was too restless, Haraszthy set off on an expedition to Central America, where he disappeared, last rumored to have been the perfect food pairing for a discerning alligator.

By the 1880s, the California wine industry was a huge success, with over eight hundred wineries growing over three hundred different *vinifera* varieties, including French Colombard (the most widely planted vine in California until Chardonnay's total acreage surpassed it in the early 1990s), Carnelian, Emerald Riesling, Green Hungarian, Ruby Cabernet, and Symphony. Chardonnay, Cabernet Sauvignon, Merlot, and Pinot Noir were then merely glimmers in yet unborn vintners' marketing schemes.

The bright California sunshine was darkened by the moral storm clouds of the Temperance Movement that were gathering on the horizon. The anti-alcohol movement gave birth to the Prohibition Party in 1869, the Woman's Christian Temperance Union in 1874, and the Anti-Saloon League in 1895. If moral piety and ax-wielding Prohibitionists weren't enough, phylloxera struck during the last two decades of the nineteenth century, devastating the vineyards and nearly ruining the California wine industry.

With the discovery of phylloxera-resistant rootstocks, the industry fought back, only to be dealt a near mortal blow just a few years later by the ratification of the Eighteenth Amendment and the start of Prohibition.

The repeal of the Eighteenth Amendment by passage of the Twenty-first Amendment in December 1933 was celebrated with toasts across the country. Unfortunately, the damage done to the California wine industry couldn't be repaired overnight. Not only was the industry in disarray, but Americans had discovered the pleasures of cocktails and hard liquor.

It was not until the 1960s, when more than half of Napa Valley had been planted with prunes, nuts, and other nongrape crops, that California began its comeback. Choosing France as their model, the new vintners, a mix of wealthy, second-career romantics and the back-to-the-earth crowd, planted Chardonnay and Cabernet Sauvignon grapes. Their vision and faith in California received validation in 1976 when Steven Spurrier, an English wine merchant, held a taste-off in Paris—California versus France. He invited the top French wine critics but led them to believe that only French wines were to be tasted. The results were earth-shattering, as the winners were Stag's Leap Cabernet Sauvignon 1973 and Chateau Montelena Chardonnay 1973. California was now a player. The wine business took on glamour, and consumers interested in the good life began to turn to wine.

# THE LAW

Wine and the law, as you have personally discovered, orbit around twin poles in the United States: tax revenue and societal control. It is thus no surprise that the BATF (Bureau of Alcohol, Tobacco, and Firearms) regulates the manufacture and marketing of wine (right down to what you can say or depict on your label), while the IRS (Internal Revenue Service) collects the taxes.

With ratification of the Twenty-first Amendment, Prohibition was repealed and control of the sale of alcoholic beverages was given to the states. The result is that today, over sixty-five years later, anyone selling wine on a national basis has fifty different sets of laws, rules, and regulations to navigate. And you've only run afoul of one state. The real question is, what was the motivation behind the indictment?

The state's public spin is that you were indicted to protect the underage from the evil influence of demon rum (oops, wine) via the ease of mail-order buying. The real reason you were indicted is that, while the state certainly isn't adverse to collecting more tax revenue, the mail-order distribution of wine directly to consumers threatens the power and profitability of influential established interests—the state-level distributors (the middle men) of wine and liquor who stand to lose the most. The distributors are the ones who are most threatened, and the felony law was partly a result of their lobbying the state legislature to protect their profitable position as the middlemen in the three-tier system.

# ANDRÉ TCHELISTCHEFF (1901–1994),
# THE FATHER OF MODERN CALIFORNIA WINE

*In 1938, André Tchelistcheff produced Beaulieu Vineyard's first Georges de Latour Private Reserve Cabernet Sauvignon and established the benchmark of quality for all California wines. Born in Moscow, he fought with the White Russian army during the Russian Revolution and, at age thirty-six, came late to the study of wine. In California, Tchelistcheff instituted improved winery hygiene, new fermentation techniques, and viticultural practices. His widespread influence as a pioneering winemaker and consultant has had a profound effect on contemporary winemakers. Rob Davis, winemaker at Jordan Vineyard & Winery, worked closely with Tchelistcheff for nearly twenty years and remembers him fondly:*

*"It was 1976. I was twenty-two and fresh out of Davis, and here was the man who almost single-handedly helped the California wine industry come of age. I was fresh clay in his hands. He was my mentor and he guided my growth as a winemaker.*

*"While André helped me with the technical aspects of winemaking, his most important influence was on my palate. He taught me how to taste. His greatest strength was his own palate. He had an amazing ability to taste and analyze an unfinished wine, to focus in on each stage of development, how the wine tasted then and how it would taste years later. He truly had the gift to penetrate the soul of a wine.*

*"He taught me to recognize and appreciate balance and finesse over muscularity. This was at a time when the fashion was for dense, overextracted, tannic reds. And here we were at Jordan crafting these elegant, drinkable wines. But he knew, and he wasn't surprised in the least when the fashion switched to the style of wines we were making. He taught me that wine is the logical extension of grapes. He always said that 'good grapes make winemakers look like geniuses.' And he also taught me the difference between maturity (balanced grapes) and ripeness (as measured in the laboratory). He made me taste the grapes and insisted that I make the decision to harvest not solely on sugar measurements but on the actual taste of the grapes—their flavor, acidity, tannins, and balance.*

*"I miss tasting with André most. He taught me to appreciate the mystery and poetry of wine. And he was a poet in his own right, whether describing a vineyard as 'a jewel of ecological elements' or the layers of flavor in a wine as 'petticoats of complex flavors.' I do miss him, but I know that he's beside me all the time, in the vineyard and in the winery."*

*Michael Bonadies*

# THE GOOD NEWS—WINE AND YOUR HEALTH

*Wine measurably drunk and in season bringeth gladness of the heart, and cheerfulness to the mind.*
**—Ecclesiastics 31:28**

*Nothing more excellent or valuable than wine was ever granted by the gods to man.*
**—Plato**

*Good wine is a daily necessity for me.*
**—Thomas Jefferson**

The good news from medical researchers is that the moderate consumption of wine contributes to improved health. This revelation burst on the scene with the CBS News/*60 Minutes* broadcast on November 17, 1991, of the story of the French Paradox, which strongly suggested wine helped prevent heart disease, the number-one killer of Americans.

### What is the French Paradox?
The French diet, high in the consumption of saturated fats, should produce a high rate of heart disease. But that is not the case.

### Why?
Red wine. The study that discovered the French Paradox found that a moderate consumption of red wine with meals dramatically lowered the incidence of heart disease among the French.

### How does wine work?
Subsequent medical studies have shown that, with moderate consumption, alcohol effectively protects against heart disease. Alcohol raises levels of HDL (the good cholesterol), which helps remove the bad cholesterol (LDL) and prevents the clogging of arteries and heart attacks. Further research has shown that wine contains antioxidants, which also aid in the fight against heart disease by preventing the formation of heart-attack-causing blood clots.

# PROHIBITION

**WHAT WAS THE TEMPERANCE MOVEMENT?**

*The effort by organized forces to outlaw the sale and consumption of alcoholic beverages (including wine).*

**WAS THIS MOVEMENT EVER SUCCESSFUL?**

*Once, in 1919, with the ratification of the Eighteenth Amendment to the Constitution, which outlawed the manufacture, sale, import, and export of intoxicating beverages. (Whatever happened to the "pursuit of happiness"?)*

**WHAT WAS PROHIBITION?**

*The period known in American history as Prohibition lasted from 1920 until 1933, the years that the Eighteenth Amendment had effect as law.*

**DID THE EIGHTEENTH AMENDMENT WORK?**

*No. Consumption of alcohol actually rose during this period, thanks to the efforts of Al Capone and other bootleggers. The net effect of the Eighteenth Amendment, which was repealed in 1933, was to give birth to organized crime.*

**WHAT WERE THE OTHER EFFECTS OF PROHIBITION?**

*Besides increased consumption of alcohol per capita, the birth of organized crime, and gangster movies, Prohibition encouraged the following creative responses to loopholes in the Volsted Act (the law that defined how the Eighteenth Amendment would be enforced):*

1. *The permission granted for the manufacture and sale of wine for religious ceremonies gave birth to the greatest call to religious vocations in the history of Christianity.*

2. *The permission granted for the manufacture and sale of wine for medicinal purposes made doctors and pharmacists very popular.*

3. *The permission granted to the heads of households to make wine at home (up to 200 gallons annually) caused California vineyards to double in*

*acreage. Unfortunately, most of the expansion was in decidedly inferior varieties (i.e., Thompson Seedless grapes).*

## WHAT SPARKED THE RISE OF THE TEMPERANCE MOVEMENT?

*Historians link the Temperance Movement to a uniquely American social phenomenon known as the Great Awakening. The Great Awakening has cyclically occurred in America in response to periods of social upheaval and fluctuating values, with alcohol often viewed as a threat to society's stability.*

- *First Great Awakening: Occurred in New England in the late 1600s and early 1700s. Witches were tried and executed. Alcohol was still okay.*
- *Second Great Awakening: Following the Revolutionary War, alcohol was blamed as the root of all social problems. The solution, to tax alcohol (the first sin tax), resulted in the Whiskey Rebellion in 1794.*
- *Third Great Awakening: The years leading up to the Civil War. Alcohol quickly took a backseat to the evil of slavery as the pressing social issue of the day.*
- *Fourth Great Awakening: Brought the Eighteenth Amendment and Prohibition into being.*
- *Fifth Great Awakening: We are in the midst of it today, as the anti-alcohol forces (known as neo-Prohibitionists) attempt to limit the availability and acceptance of alcohol (including wine) through higher taxation, legislation, and a deliberate campaign of disinformation. Witness the lifestyle police and their attempt to interfere with our pursuit of happiness not only by constantly telling us what they believe is good for us but also by trying to enact it into law.*

## IS THERE HOPE, OR ARE WE ON OUR WAY TO A SECOND PROHIBITION?

*There is hope, especially as study after study prove the health benefits of including wine in our daily diet. If there is anything Americans can get more worked up over than social issues and ills, it is their own health. So, don't forget to vote. It is very likely that the Eighteenth Amendment was ratified because thousands and thousands of able-bodied thirsty male voters just happened to be overseas fighting World War I and saving democracy.*

The antioxidants in wine are phenolic compounds. These compounds, extracted during fermentation from grapes, contribute color as well as the bitter and astringent flavors in wine. The most significant wine phenolics—quercetin, catechin, and resveratrol—are found primarily in the skins of grapes. Consequently, red wine, with its longer skin contact and greater levels of extraction during fermentation, contains a higher proportion of these protective compounds than white wine. These antioxidants also help lessen the risk for certain cancers.

## How does wine work best?

Definitely with meals. One of the five healthful habits suggested by the French Paradox is to drink moderate amounts of alcohol, particularly red wine, *with* meals. A study by the Organization for Applied Scientific Research in the Netherlands reports that moderate alcohol consumption *with* meals helps suppress the formation of blood clots.

## What's moderate consumption?

One to three glasses a day with meals.

## Recent Heart-Positive Findings

- Scientists from the American Cancer Society, the World Health Organization, and Oxford University, in a study of 500,000 men and women thirty or older, found that one drink a day lowered the mortality rate by 20%, with most of the benefit coming from lower instances of coronary heart disease.
- Harvard researchers report that a moderate daily consumption of alcohol raises levels of a naturally occurring enzyme (TPA) that helps prevent heart-attack-causing blood clots.
- A study published in *The American Journal of Cardiology* found that women benefit more than men from moderate wine consumption in preventing heart disease.
- Harvard University researchers have found that moderate alcohol consumption reduces the risk of angina pectoris.
- Studies in England indicate that moderate alcohol intake is associated with reduced hypertension.
- A Danish study published in the *British Medical Journal* found that moderate alcohol consumption lowers the risk for coronary heart disease among people with high LDL (bad cholesterol) levels.

- Brazilian researchers have found that red wine helps prevent the blocking of coronary arteries.

## Other Health-Positive Findings

- Initial studies at the University of Illinois suggest that resveratrol, a substance found in grape skins and in red wine, may help in the fight against cancer by blocking carcinogens, inhibiting tumor growth, and preventing cells from turning cancerous in the first place.
- A Danish study of 13,000 people over a twelve-year period showed that people who drank three to five glasses of wine a day cut their risk of dying early, from any cause, by 50% when compared to those who abstained.
- A Howard University School of Medicine study found that very low levels of wine consumption reduce the risk of contracting age-related macular degeneration (AMD), the major cause of blindness in the elderly, by almost 50%.
- Studies by French scientists suggest that moderate wine consumption helps protect against Alzheimer's disease and dementia.
- Doctors at Indiana University and Duke University found that moderate drinking lowers the risk of heart disease and osteoporosis in the elderly and helps maintain their learning and reasoning skills.
- A study published in the *American Journal of Public Health* reports that moderate drinkers were more resistant to five strains of the common cold virus than nondrinkers.
- A study published in the journal *Alcoholism and Clinical Experimental Research* suggests that moderate consumption—three glasses of wine on a daily basis—even over a period of twenty-five years, did not significantly increase one's risk of alcohol-related liver disease.

Other recent studies suggest or demonstrate the following:

- Moderate wine consumption lessens the risk of stroke, the third leading killer in the United States.
- It decreases the likelihood that an individual under stress will get depressed, as compared either to abstainers or to abusers of alcohol.
- It is an important indicator of a higher-than-average wage and a longer life span (it's time to ask for a raise).

## United States Says Alcohol Has Health Benefits

In its new set of dietary recommendations—"Dietary Guidelines for Americans," updated

# A Glass or Two or Three a Day

*The connection between wine and health is not new. Wine was the preferred beverage for centuries because it was safer to drink than the water. And wine has played a role in medical practice since ancient times:*

- *The Egyptians employed wine-based medicines.*
- *The Greek Hippocrates, considered the father of medicine, believed that medicine should build the patient's strength through diet and hygiene. He recommended wine as a medicine, a disinfectant, and an important part of the diet.*
- *The Romans learned that wine was the most effective disinfectant for treating battle wounds.*
- *The Hebrews recognized wine as a key component of good health.*
- *From the Middle Ages up to the late 1880s, wine continued to play an important role in medical treatment, with doctors even going so far as to prescribe specific wines for certain treatments.*

in December 1995 by the U.S. Department of Agriculture and the Department of Health and Human Services—the federal government has acknowledged for the first time that moderate drinking may lower the risk of heart disease. As reported by the *New York Times* (January 2, 1996), the government also acknowledged in the report that "alcoholic beverages have been used to enhance the enjoyment of meals throughout human history." This is a dramatic change from the 1990 guidelines, which asserted that "drinking has no net health benefit" and "is not recommended." Hooray!

## Health Concerns

### Is anything in wine harmful?

The excessive consumption of wine or any other alcoholic beverage can have a harmful effect. However, there is clearly no threat to one's health from moderate drinking.

**But what about lead?**

Lead capsules have been phased out. Any lead residue left by the capsules on older bottles can be easily wiped off before pouring.

**What about the warning labels that state "Contains Sulfites"?**

First of all, sulfites are a natural by-product of fermentation. Second, the amount of sulfites used to protect wine from spoiling is far lower than the amount on much of the fruit, produce, and other foods found in your local grocery store. Finally, the number of people who actually suffer from sulfite reactions is quite small, but if you are sensitive to sulfites, you should be very careful.

**What about the connection between alcohol and breast cancer?**

While studies have suggested a link between alcohol consumption and an increased risk of breast cancer, other breast cancer researchers believe that alcohol is not a significant risk factor. However, if you are at risk for breast cancer because of family history, it's probably best to play it safe and reduce your alcohol consumption.

**What about drunk driving?**

Drunk driving kills. Don't take any chances. Don't drive drunk and risk your own life or the life of others.

# CONCLUSION—BACK IN MONTANA

As the publicity surrounding your indictment fades, the state, content to have made their point, offers you a deal: a free case of each of your wines annually for the governor during the remainder of his term and a signed movie poster for the attorney general. After conferring with your lawyer and your true love, you take the deal and immediately slash your allocation to that state's distributor.

With your legal problems resolved, you turn with your true love to more serious questions like "If we're riding off into the sunset together and can fit only one case of wine into our saddle bags, what would those twelve bottles be?"

# RESEARCH TOPICS

Look up and read more extensively about:

- the history of wine
- the history of wine in California
- Prohibition
- Thomas Jefferson

# QUESTIONS

1. Noah's longevity (he lived to the ripe old age of 950) can be attributed to:
   a) his important animal friendships
   b) his fondness for cruises
   c) wine's health benefits
   d) none of the above

2. Throughout history, societies have wrestled with the benefits and problems of alcohol. **T or F**

3. The Greeks and Romans flavored their wines with:
   a) seawater
   b) resin
   c) herbs
   d) perfume
   e) honey
   f) all of the above

4. The great monastic orders of the Middle Ages were responsible for preserving and advancing the sciences of winegrowing and winemaking. **T or F**

**5.** _____ planted the first vineyards in California.

   a) General Mariano Vallejo

   b) Ernest Gallo

   c) Junípero Serra

   d) Lewis and Clark

**6.** Thomas Jefferson successfully made wine from _vinfera_ vines in Virginia.

   **T or F**

**7.** The very first wine pioneers of California included:

   a) Charles Krug

   b) Robert Mondavi

   c) Gustave Niebaum

   d) Francis Ford Coppola

   e) Agoston Haraszthy

   f) Georges de Latour

**8.** The Temperance Movement gave birth to:

   a) happy hour

   b) the three-martini lunch

   c) Jell-O shots

   d) keg parties

   e) none of the above

**9.** Phylloxera's devastation in the late 1880s nearly ruined the California wine industry.

   **T or F**

_Sip by Sip_

**10.** The Eighteenth Amendment to the Constitution:

    a)   encouraged the growth of organized crime

    b)   outlawed the manufacture, sale, import, or export of intoxicating beverages

    c)   lasted from 1920 until 1933

    d)   made doctors and pharmacists very popular

    e)   encouraged home winemaking

    f)   all of the above

**11.** What do the initials BATF stand for? _____

**12.** The BATF:

    a)   collects taxes on alcohol

    b)   helps arm and train right-wing militias

    c)   offers subsidies to tobacco farmers

    d)   regulates the manufacture and marketing of wine

**13.** The French Paradox reflects the fact that:

    a)   Parisians are very nice to tourists

    b)   the French harbor no inferiority complexes whatsoever due to America's overwhelming military, economic, and cultural dominance

    c)   while eating a diet high in saturated fats, the French suffer a surprisingly low incidence of heart disease

    d)   French restaurants are the friendliest

    e)   none of the above

*Michael Bonadies*

**14.** Wine's health benefits are attributed to:

    a)   a moderate consumption

    b)   drinking with meals

    c)   alcohol's ability to raise levels of HDL (the good cholesterol)

    d)   the antioxidants contained in red wine

    e)   all of the above

**15.** The federal government stated for the first time in December 1995 in its "Dietary Guidelines for Americans" that moderate drinking may lower the risk of heart disease.      **T or F**

# ANSWERS

**1.** c

**2.** True

**3.** f

**4.** True

**5.** c

**6.** False

**7.** a, c, e, and f

**8.** e

**9.** True

**10.** f

**11.** Bureau of Alcohol, Tobacco, and Firearms

**12.** d

**13.** c

**14.** e

**15.** True

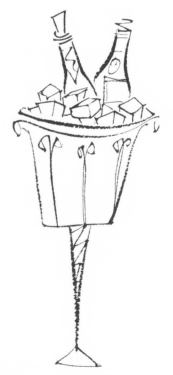

# | 9 |

# Buying, Storing, and Sharing Wine

It's a happy ending. You've eluded the law and are about to ride off into the sunset with your true love. But you want the ending rewritten. Riding off with only twelve bottles doesn't do it for you. You're the star (co-star, actually, as you have to start sharing not only your wine but equal billing with your true love) and you want more wine. You want the ending rewritten.

No way, sorry. It's time to venture into the real world of wine where you will be spending your own hard-earned money. Don't panic. It's not that difficult. If you have read this far, then the odds are that you are a hell of a lot more wine-savvy than when you started. And if you have sipped along the way, then you probably have a pretty good idea of what you like to drink. So, read on and learn some of my insider tips on how to successfully buy, store, and share wine.

## BUYING WINE

If you have in your possession three or more bottles of wine, wine is a part of your life. Whether your inventory remains constant at three bottles or increases exponentially as your curiosity grows, it's wise to view wine as a lifestyle investment. Accordingly, it is critical in developing buying strategies to take into account exactly how wine fits into your lifestyle.

### Price

First of all, what's your price point? Is it "money's no object" or one that is fiscally more restrained? Establishing a price per bottle sets a comfort level whether you are buying retail or off a restaurant winelist. If your retail comfort level is $10 to $20, you can expect to pay $20 to $40 for the same quality wine in a restaurant. Why the big jump? In a wineshop the bottle comes with a brown paper bag. Having a bottle of wine in a restaurant means that you are not cooking, serving, or doing the dishes, and if you've chosen well, it's a great-looking place. All these extras cost money, which in turn makes restaurant wine more expensive.

Once you establish your price range, you can define bargains or buys as anything below $10 retail (below $20 on a restaurant list) and indulgences as anything above $20 retail (above $40 on a restaurant list). If you want to reward yourself once in a while with a special bottle, what's your upper limit? Not sure? Then maybe a better question is, at what price do you begin to think of the mortgage, the car payments, the college loan, and your credit card limit? That's when you've hit or exceeded your comfort zone for splurges and it's time to look lower.

## Taste

Taste is paramount. It's what this book is all about—helping you discover and gain confidence in *your own taste*. Hopefully by this point, if you have been tasting as you've been reading, you have a clearer understanding of what you like in a wine and why. And most important, you are better equipped to confidently articulate exactly what you like.

Once you've established your price comfort zone, the key is to buy the wine you will enjoy. The best way to succeed is to be very clear when talking to salespeople, servers, and sommeliers about what you like or what you're in the mood to try. There are several ways to accomplish this:

## Retail

1. *Be straightforward about price.* "I'm looking for a bottle of Chardonnay for around $15." *Message:* Your comfort zone is $10 to 20.

2. *Be up-front about what you like.* "I love the Joseph Phelps Cabernet Sauvignon. Do you have something similar?" *Message:* You like a big, rich, balanced red.

3. *Take chances within reason.* "I normally buy Chardonnay, but I'd like to try a Sauvignon Blanc. What's the Chalk Hill like?
   *Message:* You've identified what you like and indicated that you want to try something new and different. By asking about a specific wine, you indicate what you are willing to spend in the search for adventure.

### Restaurant

1. *In a restaurant you can't be as blunt about price (unless you're dining alone), but you can indicate what you are willing to spend as well as how adventuresome you are.* "What's the Qupé Syrah like?

   *Message:* The price of the Qupé Syrah suggests your comfort zone, and the fact that you're asking about a Syrah indicates that you're looking for something a little different.

2. *Be up-front about what you like.* "I love the Au Bon Climat Pinot Noir. What do you have that's comparable?

   *Message:* You like Pinot Noir—a rich, complex one. And you've indicated what you're willing to spend if the Au Bon Climat Pinot Noir is on the list.


### Why Am I Buying This Bottle?

That's always a good question. Why, oh why? To impress, to be cheap, to be a big spender, to be safe, to experiment with something new, to have a wine for everyday drinking? Is the bottle for a business dinner or for a dinner with fellow wine lovers or for a celebration or for your cellar or for investment or for a gift or just because? These are all valid reasons and there are thousands more.

Knowing why you're buying a bottle certainly helps guide you to an appropriate choice, but there is nothing wrong with buying on a whim just because you like the label or remember reading something good about the producer or are in the mood for Pinot Noir or have never tasted a Viognier.


### Strategy

A smart buying strategy takes the following into account:

1. Price
2. Taste
3. Reason for purchase

Work backward to narrow down the possibilities:

1. Answer the question *why* to determine the purpose or occasion and to gain a sense of how generous or stingy you're feeling.

2. Your taste is what counts unless you're entertaining your boss. Ask yourself what you're in the mood for according to the following:
   - color: white, red, or pink
   - variety: Merlot, Cabernet Sauvignon, Pinot Noir, etc.
   - style: rich and complex or light-bodied and aromatic
   - producer: your favorite standby or a brand name or one you've only read about

3. What you're willing to spend begins to fall into place as you locate the occasion (and its importance to you) in your price comfort zone.

# BUYING RETAIL

Remember Prohibition? Well, in its wake, even over sixty-five years later, you are at the mercy of the state or county or town you live in as to how, where, and when you can buy wine. If, that is, you live in a wet town or county. If you live in a dry county, get in your car and start driving, because you're going to have to cross the county line to legally buy a bottle of wine. Unless, that is, you happen to live in the Texas Panhandle, where thirty-four counties are completely free of alcohol and New Mexico is your closest option for buying a bottle of wine.

Hopefully, you have the good fortune to live in a wet county. If you do, there are various retail venues you may find that will be more than happy to sell you a bottle of wine. Here are the pros and cons of each.

## Wineshops
These are the specialists. The guys who sell wine first and foremost.

**Pros:** When the staff is helpful, friendly, and savvy, this is where you'll have your finest retail buying experience. Typically, it offers the widest selection, the greatest price range, and the most knowledgeable service. The place to experiment and explore once you've gotten to know and trust the staff. Another plus is that wineshops, as a result of the owner's or manager's passion, often specialize in the wines of a specific region or country.

**Cons:** When the staff is elitist, snobby, and intimidating, this can be your absolute worst retail buying experience.

**Your Call:** The place to shop and learn once you've found the shop that treats you well.

# CARLO RUSSO'S TIPS FOR
# RETAIL WINE BUYING

*Carlo Russo, proprietor of Wine & Spirits World in Fort Lee, New Jersey, has turned me on to many a wonderful wine. He has advice for savvy retail purchases of California wine. He notes that the current all-time high prices reflect a series of small crops in recent California vintages that have prevented wineries from successfully meeting demand. Patience and low prices will reward those who can wait for the release of the 1997 vintage and its enormous crop. But if you must buy now:*

1. *Chardonnay, as popular as ever, presents a serious challenge in finding top quality under $15 a bottle.*
2. *Sauvignon Blanc, less expensive than Chardonnay, is often more complex and food-friendly and offers a better buy.*
3. *The lesser known varietals—Chenin Blanc, Pinot Gris, Riesling, and Gewürztraminer—offer delicious drinking at great values.*
4. *Merlot is hot, hot, hot! And the prices reflect it. It's hard to find anything good for under $10, and beware of foreign-grown Merlot in California-style packaging.*
5. *Cabernet Sauvignon maintains its collectability. Due to grape shortages, prices are up dramatically with $30 to $40 wines not uncommon. If you can, wait for the '97s and their lower prices.*
6. *Pinot Noir is the up-and-coming varietal, with tremendous improvements in quality in the past decade. If you're in the market for a silky, spicy, aromatic red at $12 to $20, try a California Pinot Noir.*
7. *California sparkling wines offer excellent drinking value in the $10 to $15 range.*
8. *Read the label to avoid foreign grapes masquerading as California juice. Look for labels that bear the words "Estate Bottled" or "Grown, Produced & Bottled by ———." The odds are that these bottles will offer greater value, since the winery didn't have to buy grapes in a very tight and expensive market, but rather grew the grapes in their own vineyards.*

**9. The following producers offer consistently good value:**

- Beaulieu
- Bogle
- Bonny Doon
- Cartlidge and Browne
- Estancia
- Fetzer
- Forest Glen
- J. Lohr
- Meridian
- Napa Ridge
- Raymond
- R. H. Phillips
- Taft Street

## State Stores

State stores are true monopolies. They are the only retail wine outlets in the most tightly regulated states. In states like Pennsylvania and Vermont, bureaucrats decide which wines you can buy.

*Pros:* The only game in town. Being bureaucrats doesn't mean they know what they're selling. As a result, you may stumble on some real steals.

*Cons:* The only game in town, with the inflated prices that come with a monopoly. A Pennsylvania resident who crosses the border into New Jersey can save 10% to 15% on wine purchases.

*Your Call:* Move.

## Package Stores

When I went away to college and tried to buy beer for the first time outside my home state of Connecticut, no one knew what I was talking about when I asked where the nearest package store was. Package stores are liquor stores; it's just that in Connecticut you couldn't leave the store without your alcoholic purchase being concealed in a package (i.e., a brown paper bag).

*Pros:* If they are less than a block away and the beer's always cold.

*Cons:* There's a reason the rest of the country calls them liquor stores and not wine stores.

*Your Call:* A trip down memory lane and your days with a fake ID.

## Supermarkets

Is the wine aisle closer to the Häagen-Dazs bars than to the potato chips? This is a very important consideration in choosing your supermarket.

*Pros:* Convenience, convenience, convenience. Grab a bottle or two along with your chips, ice cream, toilet paper, and cat food. The prices are usually the lowest in town.

# READ THE FINE PRINT

*Traitors and scoundrels! After years of promoting and preaching the quality of California wine, a number of prominent California wineries are committing vinous treason while pulling a fast one on the consumer.*

*Confronted with a wine shortage in the face of rising demand, these turncoat wineries are importing bulk wine from Chile, Argentina, and France, bottling it in California, and selling it with California-sounding brand names and California-style labels.*

*Unless you're a whiz at geography and know that Languedoc is in France, Mendoza is in Argentina, and Valle Central is in Chile, you'd better read the fine print. Take a close look at bottles $10 and under. Somewhere on the front or back label of these pseudo-California wines, in very fine print, you'll find: "Product of France," "Product of Argentina," or "Product of Chile."*

**Cons:** Limited selection, limited service, questionable storage.

**Your Call:** Love the convenience. And with a good selection under $15, you have money left over to justify taste-testing Häagen-Dazs, Starbucks, and Ben & Jerry's ice creams.

## Superstores and Discounters

Bigger boxes than the supermarket.

**Pros:** Similar to the supermarket, but often with even lower prices. This is where wineries and importers dump unsold inventory to clear the way for the release of the next vintage.

**Cons:** Same as the supermarket, and you may have to buy by the case.

**Your Call:** Love the prices and the big boxes.

## Winery Direct

Buy right at the tasting room or via mail order to cut out the middleman.

**Pros:** You may be able to buy wines you can't get back home.

**Cons:** Even though you've cut out the middleman, you are still paying full retail. No bargains here, and you have to carry the wine back home or pay for shipping. And, depending on the state you live in, you may be committing a felony.

***Your Call:*** Mixed emotions once you realize what it's costing you. If it's a wine you really want and can't get at home, then go for it.


### On-Line

The wineshop of the future?

***Pros:*** Can combine the best of wineshops and winery direct: great service (and you don't have to talk to anyone) and hard-to-find wines.

***Cons:*** You may once again be committing a felony. Nightmares of hackers stealing your credit card number or, even worse, changing the mailing address on your order and hijacking your wine.

***Your Call:*** Log on and start surfing.


### Mail-Order Catalogues

Not the catalogues mailed out by wineshops but the catalogues from the companies that want to be the mail-order giants of the wine world.

***Pros:*** The most convenient of all. Pick up the phone and order wine delivered to your doorstep. And you're probably not committing a felony either (and you were just beginning to enjoy being a hardened criminal), because many of the mail-order houses hold retail licenses in the states where they operate.

***Cons:*** You've never heard of many of the wines in the catalogue, yet all of them are lavishly praised as the next coming of Heitz Martha's Vineyard or Château Lafite-Rothschild. The scam here is that these unfamiliar wines are directly sourced, bottled, and labeled by the mail-order houses. While the wine may indeed be good, there is no way to comparison-shop to see if their price is competitive.

***Your Call:*** Buyer beware.


### Auction

Ten thousand dollars! Going once, going twice, gone to the lady in the red dress! Did your eyebrow twitch the wrong way?

***Pros:*** The opportunity to enjoy the adrenaline rush that comes with bidding on wine you really want. Bargains can be found among lesser names.

***Cons:*** It's easy to get caught up in the excitement and spend more than you want or should.

***Your Call:*** Avoid the big names and look for values.

# SEEKING VALUE

*To locate the value zone on a winelist, figure out the restaurant's average food check. To do this, add up the prices of the median-priced appetizer, entree, and dessert, and throw in a couple of bucks for coffee. This is the number that drives customer wine spending. In an expensive restaurant with an average food check of $45 to $50 per person, the values will lie below $30 on the winelist. That's because most customers are prepared to spend $35 to $50 on a bottle in order to drink a wine commensurate with the food (money talks). The wines in this lower price category are consequently slow sellers. Passion is the only justification for including them, other than to prevent a critic from reaming the restaurant in print for having a high-priced list. These are the discoveries the winelist creator is proud of and feels are worth offering to a customer to turn him or her on to something special and unique.*

*In restaurants with an average food check in the $15 to $30 range, the values lie at the higher end of the winelist. For the same reason that people spend more for wine in expensive restaurants, they spend less in cheaper restaurants. Here, the values will be found at over $30, again the slow sellers, but often the wines the person who wrote the list feels most passionate about.*

# BUYING WINE IN RESTAURANTS

The secret to restaurant wine-buying success and drinking pleasure is discovering passion. A restaurant with a passion for wine, whether the winelist offers 20 bottles or 2,000, wants to share that passion and make you happy.

### The Wine Program

While the winelist is the heart and soul of every restaurant wine program, there are other elements as well:

*By-the-Glass:* A better wine program offers the chance to sample a range of different wines at fair prices.

*Other Grape Products:* The cognacs, ports, Madeiras, sherries, and grappas.

*Training and Service:* The hallmark of a great wine program (and a great restaurant) is the service. Great service is the result of a commitment by management to teach, train, and inspire their servers about wine.

## The Winelist

Is there such a creature as the ideal winelist? Not a chance. Winelists are as individual, generous, and knowledgeable as their creators. What counts is whether or not the passion shines through and you are able to find a wine that fits your taste and price.

## Who's in charge of the winelist?

It varies from restaurant to restaurant. The person in charge may be the owner or manager or sommelier or chef or wine director or the owner's high school buddy who is now a liquor salesman. In all but the last case, the odds improve every day that the person in charge is knowledgeable and passionate about wine.

## What makes a wine list lousy?

A lack of passion and:

- gross overpricing
- a limited selection by varietal, style, or price
- lack of imagination
- lack of information (i.e., the vintages are not listed)
- misinformation (i.e., the vintages are incorrect, or the wine you want to order is not even in stock)
- lousy service

## What makes a winelist great?

Passion and:

- knowledge and the willingness to share it
- finding it fun to read
- the promise of discovery
- ease in finding what you want
- fair pricing and a range of prices that allows you to bargain-hunt or splurge
- a personality and ambition that fit the personality and ambition of the restaurant
- great service
- the realization that it's one of the reasons you want to come back

# Daniel Johnnes's Top Ten Tips for Getting the Best Restaurant Wine Experience

*Daniel Johnnes, Wine Director for the Myriad Restaurant Group, is the winner of the James Beard Foundation's 1995 Outstanding Wine Service Award and author of Daniel Johnnes's Top 200 Wines.*

1.  *Tell your server that you're interested in wine.*
2.  *Ask to speak with the sommelier or the most knowledgeable wine person on the floor.*
3.  *Ask what wines are availabe by the glass.*
4.  *Ask the sommelier/server to describe the wines by the glass.*
5.  *Ask what types of wine the sommelier/server likes, to see if you share similar tastes.*
6.  *Ask if the restaurant specializes in any particular type of wine.*
7.  *Ask if the list has any outstanding values. These can include expensive wines*
8.  *Tell the sommelier/server what types of wine you like.*
9.  *Tell the sommelier/server what your budget is.*
10. *Tip well.*

## Winelist Strategy

Buying wine in a restaurant is different from buying retail because in most restaurants:

1.  You're confronted with a smaller number of buying options.
2.  You're paying more.
3.  You may have the opportunity to buy a tightly allocated wine that you'll never see in a wineshop.
4.  Passion is infectious, and if you give in to it, you are able to discover some great new wines you never thought of trying before.
5.  You don't have to do the dishes.

What follows is an examination of the basic types of winelists you'll encounter and how to get the best out of them.

*Michael Bonadies*

## The Unabridged Encyclopedia List

The list that has everything and goes on for pages.

**Pros:** The good ones offer the chance to explore the entire world of wine at prices for every budget.

**Cons:** You could slip a disk trying to lift it or you might look up, after being engrossed in it for a half hour (and you're only halfway through), and find that your date has walked out. The bad ones are boring and way overpriced.

**Your Call:** Arrive at least a half hour before your reservation to give yourself enough time to peruse the list. Sit at the bar, have a glass of wine, and seek out recommendations from those in the know.

## The Politically Correct List

This list offers every hot, highly scored, and popular brand name you've ever read about.

**Pros:** It may offer you the chance to try a small-production wine that won't show up anywhere else in town.

**Cons:** You could have written this list by reading the *Wine Spectator* and *Wine & Spirits* every month to find out who's hot and who's scoring in the 90s.

**Your Call:** A little too predictable.

## The "Don't Give a Damn" List

Short or long, the only reason it exists is because a restaurant is supposed to have one.

**Pros:** When you're in the mood for beer.

**Cons:** Too many to list.

**Your Call:** Is the beer cold?

## The Eclectic and Quirky List

You have never heard of a single wine on this list.

**Pros:** The good ones offer passion, adventure, discovery, and very often value.

**Cons:** The bad ones are passionately one-dimensional, as one person's very subjective tastes rules, leaving anyone with a different taste out of luck.

**Your Call:** Seek passion and don't be afraid to try something new.

## The Passionate List

Short, long, or quirky, this list has something for everyone because it tries hardest to please.

***Pros:*** It's fun and easy to read and always offers a range of styles and prices.

***Cons:*** It spoils you and lowers your tolerance for winelists that lack passion.

***Your Call:*** The only way to go.

## Taking Charge

The best strategy in any restaurant is to take charge:

1. If you're not handed or offered a list on being seated, ask for it.
2. Don't be afraid to ask questions. The answers you receive will reveal the level of passion, training, and knowledge behind the list.
3. Order enough. If your party is five or more, start with two bottles.
4. Orchestrate the timing. If you intend to drink one wine with your appetizers and a second wine with your entrees, have them opened at the same time. There is nothing more frustrating than for your entrees to arrive and the wine you've chosen to be nowhere in sight.
5. Refuse hot glasses fresh from the dish-washing machine.
6. If you think a wine is bad, return it. If you're not sure, ask the sommelier to taste it.
7. If you enjoy a restaurant and its winelist, tip well and become a regular.

# SPEAK UP

*No winelist ever remains static. Wines run out of stock, vintages change, new passions are born, and customers speak up. If you'd like to see a particular wine or a greater selection of Pinot Noir or more older vintages on the list, speak up. You may be surprised by how responsive the restaurateur is to your request.*

# THE STATE OF YOUR CELLAR

You have caught the wine bug in a big way. Afternoons are spent browsing in wineshops, evenings in the easy chair reading *Wine & Spirits,* the *Wine Spectator,* the *Wine Enthusiast, The Wine Advocate,* and *Food & Wine,* and nights under the covers dreaming of all the wines you want to try. Then one morning, while making coffee in the kitchen, you glance across the

# THE JOYS OF JERSEY—BYOB

*The Garden State is famous for its tomatoes, its musical talent—Sinatra, Springsteen, and the Isley Brothers—and the joys of BYOB. Liquor licenses in New Jersey, because they are severely limited by the individual towns, are nearly an endangered species. The New Jersey restaurateur is faced with the decision either to pay big bucks for the rare license that comes up or to open for business without serving wine, beer, or liquor. The result is a boon for Jersey diners: someone else doing the dishes while they pay the same price for wine that they would if they were eating at home.*

room at your small wooden wine rack and your stash of three bottles and sigh. The yearning hits hard—you want your own wine cellar.

## What Is a Wine Cellar?

Traditionally, it was an actual cellar—below ground, with thick walls that helped to keep the wine at a fairly constant temperature and humidity. Today, a wine cellar can be a closet, a fancy-looking refrigeration unit, a high-tech wonder, or, if you're lucky, a cool, damp corner of your basement.

## What's the Big Deal with Temperature and Humidity?

A cool temperature (mid-50s) and high humidity (70%) make wine very happy as it rests on its side. Sunlight is a no-no, as is vibration, and don't forget to store the paint thinner elsewhere.

## Cellar Opportunities

Look around your domicile. What options present themselves, beyond the wooden wine rack, for satisfactory wine storage?

*Apartment:* The bedroom closet. Turn 2 to 3 cases on their sides and hide your shoes under the bed.

*Condo:* Sell the washer/dryer unit and plug in the EuroCave (that fancy refrigeration unit).

***House, with No Basement:*** The kids speak to each other for the first time in months ("I hate you!"), as you force them to share a room. Convert the vacated bedroom into a high-tech wonder of a wine cellar.

***House, with Basement:*** The cobweb-covered workbench—located in a perfect cool, damp, dark corner is history.

# CELLAR SECURITY—TAKE NO PRISONERS

*Unless your wine is stored under lock and key in a converted and booby-trapped bomb shelter built to withstand a direct nuclear hit, roommates, husbands, wives, significant others, and even the fruit of your loins pose a clear and present danger to your wine collection. Aside from the commonsense step of obtaining insurance for your collection, your only option is to live alone. But then you'd have no one to share your wine with.*

From closet to wine cellar heaven, what really matters is what you put in it, and that you eventually drink it.

## Cellar Strategies—The Old In and Out

Collector or investor, ask yourself these questions:

1. What wines do you like to drink? _____

   _____

2. What wines do you want to try? _____

   _____

3. What is your retail comfort level in regards to price per bottle?
   $ _____? to $ _____?

# THE ALLOCATION GODDESS

*So, how do you score some of the good stuff? Those hot, limited-production wines that so far you've only read or heard about but that you're dying to try. A great place to start is at the better restaurants in town, especially those with passionate winelists.*

*The problem is that there isn't enough of the good stuff to go around. Demand far exceeds the supply of many of California's best wines. Thank God for the Allocation Goddess, the nickname for the "deity" that rules in every hot winery's sales department, deciding who gets the wine and how much—and hopefully keeping everyone happy. The allocation system was designed to build brand recognition and loyalty by ensuring that limited-production wines were placed in the country's top restaurants rather than in retail shops: In a restaurant, one bottle is typically shared by four customers, while in a retail shop a single customer is likely to buy the entire case of a coveted wine.*

*Here's some advice for your favorite sommelier: Beg, plead, and grovel before the Allocation Goddess in the hope of being allowed to buy the wine. And if that doesn't work, sign up for the winery's mailing list.*

Now imagine yourself, instead of riding off into the sunset, marooned on a desert island with the true love, movie star, or celebrity of your choice. What wines would just happen to be there if you were marooned for:

**1.** The next six days? _____

_____

_____

_____

**2.** The next six months? _____

_____

_____

_____

_____

_____

_____

**3.** The next six years? _____

_____

_____

_____

_____

_____

_____

_____

It is important to envision your cellar as a reliable delivery system of drinking pleasure for the short term, the intermediate term, and the long haul. This means that the wines you purchase for your cellar should include wines for

# My Cellar

*My cellar, a former coal shed, inhabits a cool, dark, damp corner of my basement. It is 80% American and 95% red, with the reds comprised of 60% Pinot Noir, 30% Cabernet Sauvignon, and 10% other red varieties (mostly Zinfandel). It is what I like to drink. The whites in my cellar are a mix of Chardonnay, white Burgundy and Riesling, and Pinot Gris from Alsace. And, of course, there are a few bottles with bubbles tucked here and there.*

*The vast bulk of my wines—at least 99%—has been purchased because of the producer, even my everyday drinking wines, because year in and year out, regardless of vintage, the top producers make good wine. The remainder of my cellar consists of:*

- *a mixed case I buy every few weeks from my local wine merchant, Carlo Russo, who turns me on to delicious whites, reds, and rosés by sharing his passion for great value wines from the South of France and Spain.*
- *wines that I'm curious about after having read of the variety, region, or producer.*
- *wines that I buy on a whim.*

*Whenever I head down to the cellar, I try to make a determined effort not to let a wine's price—either what I paid for it or what it's worth now—prevent me from opening and sharing it. That's what wine is for, after all.*

*Michael Bonadies*

everyday drinking, wines a notch or two up for when you're in the mood to treat yourself, and special wines for just the right moment. And don't forget to save room for wines that promise adventure and discovery.

## But Which Wines?

Start with the wines you know and enjoy according to:

- color
- variety
- region
- producer
- what you like to eat

Then consider special wines that:

- you have to save for
- match birth years or anniversaries with their vintage
- evoke memories
- you wish to age

And no matter how small your cellar, save room for wines that:

- you've never heard of
- catch your fancy
- you can drink on an everyday basis without breaking the bank

## Bottle or Case?

Buy both. Buy by the case for wines you know or wines you wish to see age or appreciate. Buy by the bottle when you want to experiment and try something new. But try to avoid buying one very special bottle because:

- with everything riding on one bottle, it better not be corked, spoiled, or anything less than magical (tough odds here)

- for the amount you've spent on this one special bottle, you could have bought a case of a different wine
- you wait and wait for the perfect occasion to open this special bottle until you can't open it because it's become too valuable

## Cellar Discipline

If you don't know you have it, how can you drink it? If you do know you have it but can't find it, how can you drink it? Keep track of what you own and where it rests, either in a cellar logbook or on a computer spreadsheet.

# SERVING WINE

Wine service in a restaurant is part ritual and part theater. Serving wine at home should be much more straightforward and anxiety-free: Get out the damn cork and start pouring.

## The Gear

***Corkscrew:*** The waiter's corkscrew is the most reliable and best all-round corkscrew. It has the knife to cut the foil, the long worm to securely grip the cork without crumbling or breaking it, and the lever action to easily extract the cork. Mastering the waiter's corkscrew requires practice, which is not a bad thing, since someone has to drink the opened wine. But if you are corkscrew-challenged and despair of ever becoming one with the waiter's corkscrew, then give the Screwpull and Ah-So corkscrews a try.

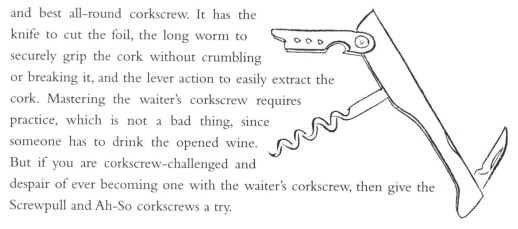

# THE CORK

Cork smells like cork. It tastes like cork too. Corks are a natural product made from the bark of cork trees native to Portugal. Inspect the length, texture, and overall quality of a cork, but don't bother smelling it. If the cork is dried and shriveled, it might indicate poor storage. If it has little holes on top, it might have been attacked by tiny worms, but this is rare. A "corked" wine is one that has been tainted by a moldy cork that most often produces a foul-smelling compound known as trichloranisole. The only way to tell if a wine is corked is to smell and taste it. If a wine is corked, it will smell and taste like wet cardboard.

The cork, being the least user-friendly closure of any consumer product known to man, can present an occasional problem. Here are the problems and some suggested solutions:

1. Problem: Corks of differing lengths, especially the longer corks found in Bordeaux and ultra-premium California bottles.

   Solution: When faced with a long cork, extract the cork a short way out of the bottle, then turn your corkscrew in a few more turns before pulling out the cork. This will help prevent broken corks.

2. Problem: When a cork breaks.

   Solution: If the remaining section of cork is still in the neck of the bottle, very gingerly reinsert your corkscrew into the cork. Turn once or twice, depending on the length of the piece remaining, and slowly and carefully pull it out.

3. Problem: When the top of a Champagne cork breaks off.

   Solution: Since Champagne is under immense pressure, the following is a dangerous procedure that must be done with utmost caution so as not to injure yourself or anyone around you. Keeping your finger over the remaining section of cork, tilt the bottle away from yourself, anyone else, and anything breakable. In one motion, remove your thumb and screw in your corkscrew. Keep the bottle titled at a 45-degree angle away from you and remove the cork.

4.  Problem: When a cork falls into the wine as the result of breaking or being pushed in.

Solution: Take a 2-foot piece of heavy string or butcher's twine. Make one big knot (about the thickness of a pencil) at one end of the string. Take a chopstick and, using its tip, guide the knot into the bottle until it is below the cork. Pull slowly on the string so that the knot catches against the bottom of the cork and pulls it up into the neck of the bottle. While maintaining tension on the string, which will keep the cork firmly in place, turn your corkscrew into the cork and then pull it out. This nearly fail-safe method requires patience and often a number of attempts before you are able to get the cork wedged back into the neck.

5. Problem: When the cork crumbles—a problem with older wines.

Solution: Decant the wine through cheesecloth or a special strainer.

It is important to remember that a cork is a natural product and its shortcomings are not necessarily a reflection of the quality of the wine it is sealing.

**Glasses:** As soon as there are more than three bottles in your cellar, it is time to spend some money on thin, hand-blown wineglasses:

**1.** The all-purpose glass

**2.** The specialized glasses

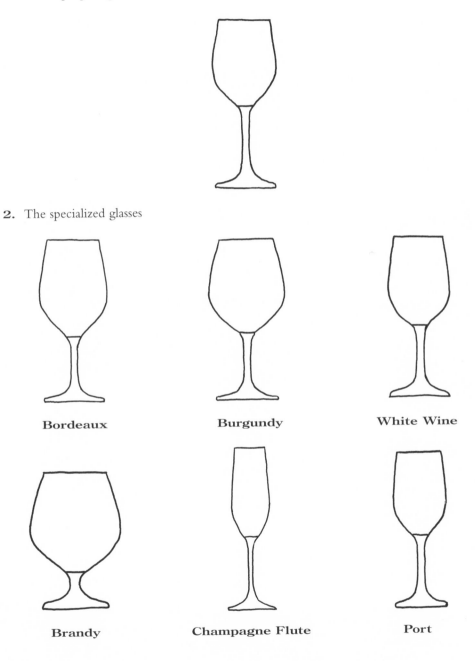

Bordeaux  Burgundy  White Wine

Brandy  Champagne Flute  Port

Glasses *do* make a difference in how a wine tastes and the pleasure it delivers. Spend the money for good glasses and buy more than you think you need, because they'll break.

*Decanter:* Decanters come in various shapes, but all serve the same purpose—to enable you to pour wine off from its sediment.

### Technique

The secret of all wine technique is to keep it simple.

*Temperature:* Serve the wine—white or red—at the temperature you most enjoy it

*Opening the Bottle:* The steps are:

1. Cut the foil below the lower lip and remove the top section. Wipe the top of the bottle with a napkin or dish towel.

2. From a 45-degree angle, aim the point of your corkscrew's worm at the center of the cork. Insert the point, moving the worm perpendicular to the cork as you begin to screw it all the way in. Catch the lever on the top lip of the bottle and slowly pull up. Using the lever action, slowly pull out the cork and then wipe the top of the bottle again.

3. Pour yourself a taste to make certain that the wine is good.

*Decanting:* You will need the following tools: decanter, corkscrew, candle, and napkin.

1. Reds must be handled more carefully than whites because they throw sediment. This is especially true of older reds and those that are unfined or unfiltered. If the bottle has been resting on its side, move it slowly to a vertical position to allow the sediment to fall to the bottom of the bottle.

2. Open the bottle as you would any other, but with greater care to keep it perfectly still. You don't want to stir up the sediment.

3. Light the candle.

4. With one hand, grasp the neck of the decanter, and with the other hand, carefully lift the bottle. Slowly tilt the bottle toward the mouth of the decanter without resting the bottle against the decanter. Position the candle under the bottle so that its light shines upward through the spot where the shoulder meets the neck of the bottle. Do not position the flame so close to the bottle that it begins to smoke.

4. Slowly and carefully pour the wine in one continuous motion into the decanter, keeping your eyes focused on the spot in the shoulder where the candle's light shines through.

5. As you near the bottom of the bottle, you will first see a stream of wispy sediment pass into the neck. It will shortly be followed by a stream of dark sediment. As soon as you see the dark sediment approach the neck, lift the bottle to stop the flow of wine.

# DECANTING TIPS

1. *Slow down and take a deep breath.*
2. *If you are decanting a very old wine, do it just prior to serving. Old reds can fade quickly.*
3. *With time and use, decanters can become spotty or cloudy. Pour a weak solution of water and bleach into the decanter and leave it overnight. The next day, rinse it thoroughly with water and it will look like new.*

# HOT WINES AND GREAT VALUES

David Gordon, Wine Director at New York City's Tribeca Grill, lists his
recommendations for hot wines and great values from California.

**Up and Coming Wineries and Their Best Wines**
Araujo Eisele Vineyard Cabernet Sauvignon and Syrah
Biale Zinfandel
Bryant Family Cabernet Sauvignon
Canepa Chardonnay
Galleron Cabernet Sauvignon
Harlan Estate Cabernet Sauvignon
Hendry Zinfandel
Landmark Chardonnay and Pinot Noir
Lewis Cellars Chardonnay and Cabernet Sauvignon
Littorai Chardonnay and Pinot Noir
Lynmar Pinot Noir
Paloma Merlot
Patz and Hall Chardonnay and Pinot Noir
Plumpjack Cabernet Sauvignon
Pride Mountain Merlot and Cabernet Franc
Selene Sauvignon Blanc and Merlot
Sine Qua Non Rhone Blends
Terraces Zinfandel

**Great Values**
Bonny Doon Pacific Rim Riesling
Buena Vista Sauvignon Blanc
Estancia Chardonnay
Hess Select Cabernet Sauvignon
Indigo Hills Pinot Noir
Liberty School Cabernet Sauvignon
Marietta Old Vine Red
Meridian Chardonnay
Markham Sauvignon Blanc
Napa Ridge Pinot Noir
Ravenswood Zinfandel Vintner's Blend
R. H. Phillips Chardonnay
Talus Merlot

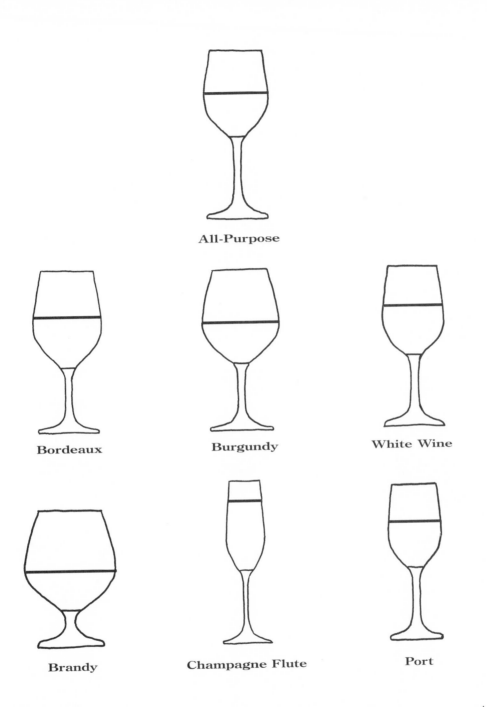

**All-Purpose**

**Bordeaux**

**Burgundy**

**White Wine**

**Brandy**

**Champagne Flute**

**Port**

***Serving Sizes:*** To provide the appropriate serving size for dinner guests means, with the exception of huge, oversized glasses, filling the wineglass just short of halfway. If you are hosting a wine tasting, it is appropriate to fill the wineglass just short of one-quarter way.

# SHARING WINE—
# HE WHO DIES WITH THE MOST WINE LOSES

Other than at a structured wine tasting, the odds are that when you share wine, it is in concert with food. Which brings up the controversy of food and wine pairings. Maybe the salmon isn't really in the mood to be paired with the Chardonnay tonight. Maybe it's feeling racy and wants to tango with the Pinot Noir. Give me a break. Sure, there is a wine out there somewhere that is the absolutely ideal match for the meal you are cooking tonight, but do you really care? And even if you did, do you have the time and energy to track it down? Eat and drink what you like!

A much more sensible and less stressful approach is to match the wine with the occasion and your guests. Here are a few examples.

### Cocktail Party

You'll need a white and a red. Your best bet is to serve your everyday white and red. That way, any wine that's left over will be consumed. Think about rosé if the party is outdoors in the warm weather.

### Brunch

If you want a fun, casual party with style, there is no better way to achieve this than by serving a sparkling wine or champagne. Buy really inexpensive sparkling wine if you plan to serve mimosas or bellinis.

### Docks and Decks

Lazy summer afternoons hanging with family and friends. Think easygoing in terms of the wine as well: rosé; light, crisp whites; and simpler, light-bodied reds.

### Chillin' and Grillin'

To start, sip a big, complex white served a little colder than normal, because it's hot outside, and when you serve the charred meat, pop open a big red.

### Vacations

If you're renting a house, pack up some of those wines you keep on finding excuses not to open. You'll have the time and space to really appreciate them.

*Michael Bonadies*

# Cellar Motives

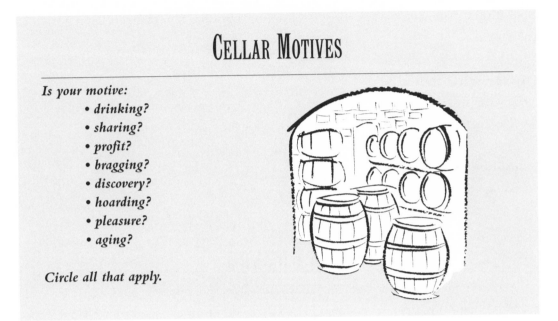

*Is your motive:*
- *drinking?*
- *sharing?*
- *profit?*
- *bragging?*
- *discovery?*
- *hoarding?*
- *pleasure?*
- *aging?*

*Circle all that apply.*

## Birthdays

Drink something really good and out of your price comfort zone. It's fun to buy vintages of Bordeaux, Port, and California Cabernet Sauvignon—wines all built to age—that match the years your children were born. Starting with the child's seventh birthday, open one bottle each year. Take notes to see how both are maturing. Just make certain you buy enough to pass on at least a few bottles when your child turns twenty-one.

## Brothers-in-Law

If they're know-it-all creeps like the mook who got shot between the eyes earlier in this book, don't even bother inviting them over. But if they're like the two great brothers-in-law I have, and to whom I apologize for making fun of brothers-in-law, bring something really good up from the cellar.

## Takeout

Go with your everyday white or red.

## Business Dinner

Unless your guests are into wine, serve wines that are in the middle of your price comfort zone. If they share your passion for wine, trade up, but stick to wines you know won't let you down.

### Dinner with Friends

Share your passion and preach the gospel. Open and pour wines you are excited about, and don't forget to share the really good stuff once in a wine.

### Romance

Sparkling wine or Pinot Noir.

# YUCK OR YUM

Yuck or yum, that's what it all comes down to. What tastes good to *you*. Champagne with burgers, Cabernet Sauvignon with salmon, White Zinfandel on a scorching summer day, a $9 bottle or a $900 bottle. Your taste is the only thing that matters, and following your taste buds is the surest route to consistent drinking pleasure.

Wine books (even this one) and magazines, wine courses and experts do not hold a lock on the truth about wine. At best, they're guides, similar to the books, magazines, and expertise you might seek in planning a vacation to a distant locale. For most of us, wine was an exotic world when we first became curious. The key to exploring the world of wine is to plunge in and experience it firsthand. There is no substitute for the experience of tasting and exploring. Then and only then are you able to arrive at a true awareness of what *you* like and enjoy in wine. So keep on sipping, and don't be afraid to stay with the wines you like or to constantly seek new taste experiences. The goal is pleasure—and achieving an ease and comfort with wine in order to make it an integral part of your daily life. Good luck, good sipping, and thanks for reading this book.

# QUESTIONS

1. What is your retail comfort level?
    a) $5 to $10
    b) $10 to $20
    c) $20 to $35
    d) $35 to $50
    e) $50+

2. What is the most you have ever paid for a bottle of wine?
    a) retail _____
    b) restaurant _____

3. The best way to buy a bottle you will enjoy is to be clear to the salesperson or server about what you like in a wine.          **T or F**

4. A dry county offers the best prices on wine.          **T or F**

5. Which of the following is least likely to be a retail wine option?
    a) state store
    b) wineshop
    c) supermarket
    d) hardware store
    e) on-line

6. What is the most important characteristic of a great wine-list? _____

7. Restaurant wine buying differs from retail wine buying because:
    a) you don't have to wash the glasses
    b) you'll pay more
    c) you'll most likely be confronted with a smaller selection

    d)   you may have the opportunity to buy a wine you'll never find in a retail store

    e)   all of the above

8. Customers should never speak up about what they'd like to see on a restaurant's winelist. **T or F**

9. Restaurant or retail, a customer should never return a bottle of wine he or she thinks is corked. **T or F**

10. Values can be found on the low end of expensive restaurants' winelists and the high end of inexpensive restaurants' winelists. **T or F**

11. BYOB is a beautiful thing. **T or F**

12. Yes or no: Do you dream of creating or expanding your wine cellar? **Yes or No**

13. Wine is for sharing. **T or F**

14. Yes or no: After reading this book, are you a more confident and knowledgeable consumer? **Yes or No**

15. What are the next three wines you want to try?

_____

_____

# THE WEDDING FEAST AT CANA

*Jesus Christ performed his first miracle when the host ran out of wine and He turned water into wine, saving the day. But then the guests dissed the host by asking why he saved the best wine for last. So take this lesson to heart and:*

1. *Don't run out. For a dinner party, play it safe and figure on about three-quarters of a bottle per person. Any opened bottles will be fine for a day or two.*

2. *Serve whites before reds, dry before sweet, light-bodied before full-bodied, young before old, and save the best for last. The only problem in following the standard order of serving wine is when the old is really old or the best is really best and there are a number of wines preceding them. By the time you get to the old or the best, your powers of perception might be shot and these great wines wasted.*

# ANSWERS

1. Your call
2. Your call
3. True
4. False
5. d
6. passion
7. e
8. False
9. False
10. True
11. True
12. Hopefully, yes
13. True
14. Hopefully, a BIG YES
15. Your call

# Appendices

## A. OTHER GRAPE PRODUCTS

Grapes are grown to make not only wine but also jams and jellys, raisins, and candies, as well as other alcoholic beverages. The following beverages are some of the other grape products sold in restaurants and wineshops.

## PORT

Port is a fortified wine made from red (and occasionally white) wine grapes in the Douro region of Portugal. Port typically undergoes a fermentation that is cut short by the addition of brandy to keep the wine sweet.

### Aging: Wood or Bottle?

A port's style is determined by its aging vessel: wood casks called pipes, or bottles.

**Wood-Aged Ports:** These ports are deliberately exposed to air as they are frequently racked from cask to cask.

*Tawny Ports:* The very finest wood-aged ports. As tawny ports age, their color lightens from deep red to amber (or tawny) and they develop aromas and flavors of nuts, dried fruits, and spices. Age-designated tawny ports are blends of different aged stock, bottled in ten-year increments, which indicate the average age of the blend (ten-year tawny, twenty-year tawny, up to forty years).

*Colheitas:* Vintage-dated tawny-style ports aged in wood for a minimum of seven years.

*Ruby Ports:* Blended wines of several harvests that receive a minimum of wood aging prior to bottling. Fruitier and rougher than tawnies.

*Premium Ruby or Propriety Blend Ports:* Ruby-style ports made from better-quality blends.

*Late-Bottled Vintage Port (LBV):* Vintage port's poor cousin. This port spends up to six years in wood before bottling. Something of a hybrid between a wood- and a bottled-aged port, LBV port is ready to drink on release.

**Bottle-Aged Ports:** These ports see a short barrel aging period before being bottled.

*Vintage Ports:* A blend of the highest-quality ports from a single vintage blended to reflect the shipper's house style. Aged in wood for two years prior to bottling, vintage ports require at least ten years in the bottle before they are ready to drink. Vintages are declared only two or three times in a decade and can produce wines capable of lasting for fifty years. While vintage ports represent a very small percentage of total port production, their quality and ability to age make them the kings of the port world.

*Single-Quinta Vintage Port:* Made the same way as vintage port, except that all the grapes come from a single estate, or quinta. These ports tend to be produced in good years that fail to merit being declared a vintage, although more and more producers are making them nearly every year.

# SHERRY

Sherry is a fortified wine produced in southern Spain. The word "sherry" is an English corruption of Jerez, one of the important towns involved in the production of sherry.

Sherry is a white wine whose special flavors and characteristics can be attributed to three things:

1. The *flor* yeast that gives fino sherry its distinctive flavor and aroma.
2. Following fermentation, the fortification of sherry with brandy to raise its alcohol content to 17% to 20% (table wines average 11% to 14% alcohol). It is then aged in oak casks.
3. The *solera* system, which is a method of blending and aging. In sherry houses, wine casks are stacked vertically. The oldest blends of sherry are at the bottom; each cask above is progressively younger. When sherry is removed from the bottom cask to be bottled (never more than 20% at a time), it is replaced by wine from the cask immediately above it, which is, in turn, replaced by wine from the cask above it, and so on all the way to the top.

## Styles of Sherry

**Fino:** Pale yellow in color. Dry and elegant. An excellent aperitif.

**Manzanilla:** Similar to fino but lighter.

**Amontillado:** A fino that has been allowed to age in the *solera* system and takes on a darker color and a nutty flavor.

**Oloroso:** A sherry that is not affected by the *flor* yeast during fermentation. With age, it becomes more complex in terms of flavor and aroma. Can be dry or sweet.

**Palo Cortado:** A very rare sherry that is, stylistically, between an amontillado and an oloroso.

**Pedro Ximénez or Cream Sherries:** Sweet sherries in which the brandy is added during fermentation to ensure a specific sugar level in the finished wine. These sherries are dark in color and can vary in degree of sweetness.

# MADEIRA

Madeira is the name of a Portuguese island off the coast of Morocco. The fortified wine produced there, Madeira, is the world's longest-living wine. Madeira was one of the most popular wines in the American colonies and was used to toast the signing of the Declaration of Independence. Subsequently, Madeira fell out of favor and is just now beginning to make a comeback.

Madeira is produced according to the *estufa* system, in which finished wines are artificially aged by means of heat and extended barrel aging for up to twenty years.

## Styles of Madeira

Madeira has been traditionally named after its principal grape varieties, all of which are known for their high levels of acidity.

**Sercial:** A dry Madeira with a nutty aroma.

**Verdelho:** Medium-dry with a smokey flavor.

**Bual:** Sometimes spelled Boal; sweeter and richer than Sercial or Verdelho.

**Malmsey:** The sweetest and longest-lived Madeira, known for its tremendous richness and concentration of flavor

# COGNAC

The world's most famous brandy is produced in the southwest of France. Cognac is made from Ugni Blanc grapes (also known as Trebbiano). Following fermentation, the wine is distilled as soon as possible in a pot still. The distilled cognac is aged in French oak barrels, blended, and then bottled.

**Styles of Cognac**

*V.S.:* All the cognac in the blend must be at least three years old.

*V.S.O.P.:* All the cognac in the blend must be at least five years old.

*X.O., Napoleon, and Extra:* There is no guarantee of age with these Cognacs, but they tend to be considerably older than a V.S.O.P.

# ARMAGNAC

Armagnac is a brandy produced in Gascony in southwest France. Armagnac differs from cognac in that when it is well made, it results in a richer, fuller brandy.

# GRAPPA

Grappa, which is known in France as marc, is a brandy that is made from pomace. Pomace is the term for the mass of skins and seeds left over from the winemaking process.

# OTHER BRANDIES

Excellent brandies are also produced in Spain and the United States.

# VERMOUTH

Vermouth is a fortified wine, of many different styles and names, that has been flavored with herbs.

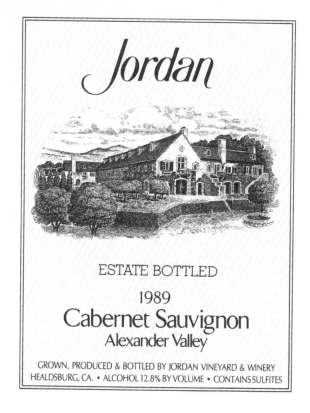

**ESTATE BOTTLED**

**1989**

**Cabernet Sauvignon**

Alexander Valley

GROWN, PRODUCED & BOTTLED BY JORDAN VINEYARD & WINERY
HEALDSBURG, CA. • ALCOHOL 12.8% BY VOLUME • CONTAINS SULFITES

**B. How to Read a Label**

1. The name of the producer.

2. "ESTATE BOTTLED." By law the wine must meet the following conditions:

    a) The wine must have a viticultural area appellation (Alexander Valley).

    b) The winery must be located in the viticultural area.

    c) The winery must have grown 100% of the grapes used to make the wine on land owned or controlled by the winery within the viticultural area of appellation. "Controlled" means a lease of at least three years' duration.

    d) The winery must have crushed the grapes, fermented the resulting must, and finished, aged, and bottled the wine in a continuous process.

3. The vintage year. The year in which the grapes were harvested. 95% of the grapes must have been harvested in that year.

4. The grape varietal. Seventy-five percent of the wine must come from Cabernet Sauvignon.

5. The appelation of origin. In this case, the AVA (Approved Viticultural Area) is Alexander Valley, which is located in Sonoma County.

6. "GROWN, PRODUCED & BOTTLED BY" must follow the same conditions as "ESTATE BOTTLED" in this case.

7. The address of the winery.

8. The alcohol content by volume. Table wines must be between 7% and 13.9%, with an allowable allowance of 1.5%.

9. Since 1987, wines containing more than 10 parts per million of sulfur dioxide (which means nearly all wines, since many yeast strains produce that much during fermentation) have to carry the statement "CONTAINS SULFITES."

In this case, Insignia is a proprietary name that Joseph Phelps uses for several reasons. One legal reason is that they cannot call the wine one specific varietal unless it is 75% or more of that one grape. Therefore, the blend of grapes in Insignia can change from year to year, giving the winemaker the option to use the blend he decides on. In this case, the blend of grapes is specified on the label, but that is not mandatory by law.

"TABLE WINE" is a term that may be used in place of giving the actual alcohol content for wines 14% or less.

# VINTAGE CHART

| REGION (YEAR) | '78 | '79 | '80 | '81 | '82 | '83 | '84 | '85 |
|---|---|---|---|---|---|---|---|---|
| CALIFORNIA RED | 90 | 82 | 87 | 85 | 86 | 78 | 90 | 95 |
| CALIFORNIA WHITE | 85 | 83 | 88 | 87 | 86 | 87 | 88 | 84 |
| BORDEAUX | 88 | 86 | 73 | 85 | 96 | 87 | 72 | 89 |
| BURGUNDY | 89 | 89 | 80 | 85 | 74 | 82 | 84 | 77 |
| RHÔNE | 95 | 87 | 84 | 83 | 85 | 88 | 76 | 90 |
| CHAMPAGNE | NV | 88 | NV | 83 | 90 | 85 | NV | 86 |
| PIEDMONT | 94 | 87 | 72 | 81 | 93 | 78 | 64 | 94 |
| TUSCANY | 87 | 76 | 70 | 83 | 88 | 82 | 64 | 93 |
| GERMANY | 73 | 84 | 68 | 83 | 80 | 91 | 72 | 86 |

Rating: 90–100 Excellent, 80–89 Very Good, 70–79 Average, 60–69 Below Average

# GOVERNMENT WARNING LABEL

On November 18, 1989, a rule went into effect requiring the labels of all alcoholic beverages sold in the United States to carry the following statement:

> GOVERNMENT WARNING: (1) ACCORDING TO THE SURGEON GENERAL, WOMEN SHOULD NOT DRINK ALCOHOLIC BEVERAGES DURING PREGNANCY BECAUSE OF THE RISK OF BIRTH DEFECTS. (2) CONSUMPTION OF ALCOHOLIC BEVERAGES IMPAIRS YOUR ABILITY TO DRIVE A CAR OR OPERATE MACHINERY, AND MAY CAUSE HEALTH PROBLEMS.

This warning is usually found on the back of the bottle toward the bottom. It does have to be a certain readable size by law designated by the BATF.

The wine industry is concerned about these statements because they do not say anything about how much wine may produce these results.

This vintage chart has been created by David Gordon, Wine Director at New York's TriBeCa Grill.

| '86 | '87 | '88 | '89 | '90 | '91 | '92 | '93 | '94 | '95 | '96 |
|-----|-----|-----|-----|-----|-----|-----|-----|-----|-----|-----|
| 92 | 90 | 78 | 84 | 92 | 91 | 90 | 91 | 95 | 93 | 92 |
| 90 | 76 | 89 | 85 | 90 | 87 | 89 | 90 | 91 | 92 | 89 |
| 92 | 79 | 90 | 97 | 92 | 75 | 78 | 84 | 89 | 93 | 91 |
| 95 | 83 | 86 | 91 | 94 | 82 | 83 | 88 | 83 | 92 | 90 |
| 84 | 78 | 91 | 95 | 92 | 80 | 82 | 85 | 89 | 91 | 88 |
| 85 | NV | NV | 90 | 85 | NV | NV | NV | NV | 88 | 91 |
| 80 | 84 | 92 | 93 | 94 | 77 | 74 | 87 | 85 | 90 | 93 |
| 85 | 76 | 91 | 72 | 91 | 75 | 77 | 76 | 84 | 92 | 80 |
| 80 | 83 | 89 | 89 | 95 | 86 | 88 | 87 | 90 | 88 | 88 |

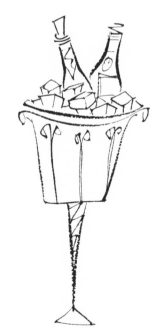

*Sip by Sip*

# Bibliography

Many of the following books and magazines were important sources I used in writing this book. All of these books and magazines below will be helpful in your continuing wine education.

## Books

Anderson, Burton. *The Wine Atlas of Italy.* Simon & Schuster, 1990.

Baldy, Marian, *The University Wine Course.* The Wine Appreciation Guild, 1993.

Darlington, David. *Angel's Visits.* Henry Holt, 1991.

De Villiers, Marq. *The Heartbreak Grape.* HarperCollins, 1994.

Halliday, James. *Wine Atlas of California.* Viking, 1993.

Johnnes, Daniel. *Daniel Johnnes's Top 200 Wines.* Penguin, 1996.

Johnson, Hugh. *Encyclopedia of Wine.* Simon & Schuster, 1985.

———. *World Atlas of Wine.* Simon & Schuster, 1994.

Johnson, Hugh, and Halliday, James. *The Vinter's Art.* Simon & Schuster, 1993.

Kramer, Matt. *Making Sense of Burgundy.* Morrow, 1990.

———. *Making Sense of California Wine.* Morrow, 1992.

Lynch, Kermit. *Adventures on the Wine Route.* Farrar, Straus & Giroux, 1988.

Parker, Robert M., Jr. *Bordeaux.* Simon & Schuster, 1991.

Robinson, Jancis. *The Oxford Companion to Wine.* Oxford University Press, 1994.

———. *Vines, Grapes, Wines.* Knopf, 1986.

Rosengarten, David, and Wesson, Joshua. *Red Wine with Fish.* Simon & Schuster, 1989.

Spurrier, Steven. *Académie du Vin Guide to French Wines, Revised and Updated*. Macmillan, 1991.

Sutcliffe, Serena. *Champagne*. Simon & Schuster, 1988.

Thompson, Bob. *The Wine Atlas of California and the Pacific Northwest*. Simon & Schuster, 1993.

Wagner, Philip M. *Grapes into Wine*. Knopf, 1984.

Zraly, Kevin. *Windows on the World Complete Wine Class*. Dell, 1985.


## MAGAZINES

*Fine Wine Folio*. Holland & Edwards Publishing, Inc., 250 Mercer Street, A203, New York, NY 10012

*International Wine Cellar* (Tanzer Business Communications, Inc., P.O. Box 20021, Cherokee Station, New York, NY 10021)

*The Wine Advocate;* phone: (410) 329-6477

*Wine & Spirits;* phone: (212) 695-4660

*Wine Enthusiast;* phone: (800) 356-8466

*Wine Spectator;* phone: (800) 752-7799

# Organizations

The following organizations are involved in the promotion of wine as a civilized beverage:

American Beverage Institute (ABI)
607 14th Street NW
Suite 1110
Washington, DC 20005
Phone: (202) 347-5215
Fax: (202) 347-5250

The American Institute of Wine & Food (AIWF)
1550 Bryant Street
Suite 700
San Francisco, CA 94103
Phone: (415) 255-3000
Fax: (415) 255-2874

Wine Institute
425 Market Street
Suite 1000
San Francisco, CA 94105
Phone: (415) 512-0151
Fax: (415) 442-0742

# Index

*Index*

**211**